The Ice Cube Is Melting

D1503021

LYLE E. SCHALLER

The Ice Cube Is Melting

What Is Really at Risk in United Methodism?

Abingdon Press
Nashville

THE ICE CUBE IS MELTING
WHAT IS REALLY AT RISK IN UNITED METHODISM

Copyright © 2004 by Abingdon Press

All rights reserved.

No part of this work may be reproduced or transmitted in any form or by any means, electronic or mechanical, including photocopying and recording, or by any information storage or retrieval system, except as may be expressly permitted by the 1976 Copyright Act or in writing from the publisher. Requests for permission can be addressed to Abingdon Press, P.O. Box 801, 201 Eighth Avenue South, Nashville, TN 37202-0801, or emailed to permissions@abingdonpress.com.

This book is printed on acid-free paper.

Library of Congress Cataloging-in-Publication Data

The ice cube is melting : what is really at risk in United Methodism / Lyle E. Schaller.

  p. cm.
  Includes bibliographical references.
  ISBN 0-687-33881-6 (alk. paper)
  1. United Methodist Church (U.S.)—Membership. I. Schaller, Lyle E.

  BX8382.2.Z5I34 2004
  287'.6—dc22

                             2004000852

All scripture quotations are taken from the *New Revised Standard Version of the Bible,* copyright 1989, by the Division of Christian Education of the National Council of the Churches of Christ in the United States of America. Used by permission. All rights reserved.

04 05 06 07 08 09 10 11 12 13—10 9 8 7 6 5 4 3 2 1

MANUFACTURED IN THE UNITED STATES OF AMERICA

To
Bill and Erma

CONTENTS

FOREWORD

by Adam Hamilton

I am proud and grateful to be a United Methodist pastor. I believe I represent a large portion of our denomination's clergy and laity who stand somewhere between the conservatives on our right and the liberals on our left, holding tenaciously to the *via media*—the middle way. I have never attended an event sponsored by, nor joined any of the "conservative renewal movements" described in Leon Howell's *United Methodism @ Risk*. Neither have I joined any caucuses, attended any events, or signed any documents sponsored by groups on the left in our denomination. I have been interviewed by both *Good News* and by *The Christian Century* in the last year. And, like many in our denomination, I both appreciate, and get frustrated with, those on the left and the right.

I bought my copy of *United Methodism @ Risk* at annual conference, thinking it was another book about how we might revitalize our denomination. (I had always referred to this as the "renewal" of our denomination until reading *@ Risk* where I discovered that this word is seen as synonymous with the conservative movement!) The revitalization of our church is a great passion of mine, and of many of my colleagues in the theological and sociological center of our denomination. I believe that United Methodists have an approach to the gospel that twenty-first–century people will respond to and are, in fact, hungry for, if only we could be clear about what this is.

I was a bit surprised when I began reading @ *Risk* and found that it wasn't a strategic look at how we might create a thriving denomination in the future. Instead it was an attack upon the conservative wing of our church and an exposé of what is portrayed as a plot to gain control of our denomination by conservatives.

Looking over the list of names associated with the book, I recognized several persons I respect and hold in high regard. But I found the approach of the book a bit surprising. It decried the conservative methods of attacking those persons on the left in our church. It denounced the demeaning tactics of the right. But too often the book seems to take up this same approach in its description and assessment of United Methodist conservatives. It seemed to me, as a reader standing somewhere between the left and the right, that the book was one more salvo in a cultural and theological war where both sides seem to talk past one another, and neither has truly understood the other.

A more helpful approach to this issue, at least as a starting point, would be for each side to recognize and understand the feelings and concerns of the other. For those on the left, is it possible to understand why conservatives are upset when leaders in The United Methodist Church seem to lay aside the "essential" doctrines of the Christian faith? Is there a way to value the role of conservatives in helping to keep us anchored to the Bible and the gospel, and to appreciate that their challenges may be, in an unusual sort of way, a gift? Can we be grateful for the passion of many conservatives around renewing the church without necessarily buying the conservative agenda, hook, line, and sinker?

Many of the conservatives I know in our denomination are fine people from whom I have a lot to learn. Most are not mean-spirited. Most are thoughtful and informed. And most would be considered moderates, or even liberals, in truly conservative denominations. Finally, many are nervous about the future of our church, and they feel they have been on the outside in a denomination that seems to them to be controlled by the left. They feel disempowered, outmaneuvered, and disrespected.

For those on the right, in the conservative movements in our church, is it possible to understand why @ *Risk* was written? Can we not understand that when we personally attack others, when love is no longer seen in our words or actions, when we fail to find anything to value or appreciate in our brothers and sisters on the left, then rather than positively influencing these persons we push them further from the positions and ideas we believe are important? Too often conservatives have come across as judgmental, unkind, and self-righteous. Having received letters from fundamentalists through the years who questioned my faith, my motives, and my sanity, I can appreciate the tone of @ *Risk*—it is the approach and tone I have often wanted to take with those who have hurt me by their pronouncements.

Many of the liberals I know are deeply devoted to Christ, read and study the Scriptures, spend time on their knees daily in prayer, and truly want to see their churches grow, reach unchurched people, and lead them into a vital and life-transforming relationship with Jesus Christ. They have felt attacked by conservatives in their own congregations and, by implication, in some of the words and work of the renewal movements. And they fear conservatives organizing and planning to gain an increasing share of control of our denomination.

In this book, Lyle Schaller has identified many of the "lines in the sand" that divide United Methodists. He has, with his satirical wit and challenging propositions, laid out a host of options for resolving this battle between conservatives and liberals in The United Methodist Church. And he has with his series of rapid-fire questions forced us to think about what we believe, what we are doing, what we really want, and the probable outcomes of the direction we are currently headed.

For those looking for one easy and simple solution to our problems, this book will disappoint. Lyle did not intend to provide *the* answer. His intention was to "flood the system" with information, probing questions, and possibilities. Yet throughout the book, he makes statements that point us toward what may be pieces of the puzzle of the future of our church. Have your highlighter ready. Words like "dysfunctional" and "outcomes" and "exit fee" and "trust" are among many you will want to ponder. As I read Lyle's book, I could hear my father, speaking when I was a teenager about to make a very bad decision, saying, "Go ahead. If you really think this is what you should be doing, go ahead and do it. But remember, here are a few of the implications of your decision. . . . " His willingness to push me, the freedom he gave me to make a bad decision, and his reminder of the implications of the course of action I was about to take, ultimately kept me from making the wrong decision.

Hegel spoke of the progression of ideas throughout history in terms of thesis, antithesis, and synthesis. If the conservatives in The United Methodist Church have offered us a thesis, and those represented by the authors of *United Methodism @ Risk* have offered us the antithesis, I believe it is time for those in the center of our denomination to, in partnership with those on the left and right, formulate a new synthesis; one that takes seriously the concerns on the right and the left, which is able to draw upon the strengths of each, and which forges an even stronger and healthier United Methodism for the twenty-first century. I believe, in the end, this is what Lyle Schaller is pointing us toward.

Adam Hamilton is the founding pastor of The United Methodist Church of the Resurrection in Leawood, Kansas. That congregation was founded in 1990. Twelve years later this new mission was averaging more than 6,000 at weekend worship. It stands out as a model of a high-expectation congregation and of how a mainline Protestant church outside the Sunbelt can thrive in the twenty-first century.

INTRODUCTION

Occasionally it is possible to point back to the day and the experience that motivated an author to write a book. On July 23, 2003, I read *United Methodism @ Risk: A Wake-up Call*, by Leon Howell.[1] (Subsequent references to this volume simply will be @ *Risk*.)

My immediate reaction was, this is an exceptionally important book! It draws two clear lines in the sand and also raises other crucial issues. One line in the sand reflects the differences in biblical interpretation, which I am labeling, in a great oversimplification of reality, "conservative" and "progressive." This is *not* a new debate! This distinction between turning to Scripture or to human reason as the ultimate source of authority has been around for centuries, sometimes defined as the difference between Jerusalem and Athens.[2]

This classical metaphor defined as citizens of Jerusalem those Christians who turn to Scripture and tradition as the two primary sources of authority in their religious pilgrimage. By contrast, the residents of Athens place a high value on reason and learning as they search for meaning in life. Those who declare, "I give equal weight to Scripture, tradition, reason, learning, and experience in defining the Christian faith" constitute a third category. Occasionally they are identified as "wanderers in the wilderness" by those on a self-identified spiritual journey. These pilgrims go on to explain that their search is for certainty, not ambiguity.

One popular solution to the current clash in The United Methodist Church over the sources of authority for interpreting the Christian faith to both believers and nonbelievers is that this denomination can and should resemble a huge tent with plenty of room under it for migrants from both Athens and Jerusalem as well as those now wandering in the wilderness. A theologically pluralistic denomination should be inclusive and accommodate everyone.

That also is *not* a new idea![3]

The most highly visible experience with this both-and solution has been in what originally were organized as Christian colleges and universities.[4] As the years and decades rolled by, the teams from Athens won nearly every contest. One of the big contests was over the criteria to be used in evaluating the school. Two of the early criteria were (1) "Are we attracting students from our churches?" and (2) "Are we able to raise the money we need to pay our bills?"

Eventually the folks from Athens took over the responsibility for deciding on the criteria for evaluation. Among the top criteria on their list were (1) the academic credentials of the faculty, (2) the books and journals in the library, (3) the compensation for faculty, (4) the weekly classroom work load for the faculty, (5) the quality of the physical plant, and (6) the academic records of entering students. Gradually, the leaders from Athens were able to win this contest. The crucial step in building a great institution of higher education is to bring together a group of scholars with earned reputations as outstanding researchers.

On the losing side of that debate were those, including some from Athens and many from Jerusalem, who agreed, "Our system of evaluation looks at outcomes, not inputs. Our number-one criterion for evaluating any institution of higher education can be condensed into a simple question. Twenty years after graduation, what proportion of the graduates look back with deep gratitude and reflect, 'That is where I first discovered the joy of learning. That was the place, and those were the teachers who challenged me and equipped me to become a lifelong learner. They opened the door for me to a world I had not known existed. That experience transformed my life!' The dissenters will argue that is the responsibility of the high school, not the university. We wish that were true, but most large public high schools prepare a tiny minority of the seventeen-year-old males to earn an athletic scholarship while the majority learn how to be bored but not yielding to the temptation to engage in violent antisocial behavior."

If that were the end of the contests between Athens and Jerusalem, the reader might shrug and comment, "That's interesting, but I thought this was to be a book about contemporary American Protestantism."

Several big tents have been erected in that park called The Home of American Protestantism. On one side of that park are the ice cubes described in chapter 1. On the other side are several tents of various sizes. A midsize tent houses the Unitarian Universalist Association. A guide explains, "We try to be inclusive. We welcome three groups of people. We welcome those who believe in the existence of a Supreme Being. We welcome those who do not believe in a Supreme Being. We also welcome those who welcome both believers and nonbelievers."

One of the largest tents in this park houses the congregations and other organizations that constitute the United Church of Christ (UCC). A huge sign in the middle of the tent reproduces the second paragraph of the UCC constitution. The first two sentences read as follows: "The United Church of Christ acknowledges as its sole Head, Jesus Christ, Son of God and Savior. It acknowledges as kindred in Christ all who share in this confession."

Facing it is a sign that reproduces paragraph 18 of Article V of the UCC Constitution. This paragraph guarantees the complete and unreserved autonomy of each congregation including the right "to formulate its own covenants and confessions of faith." This is clearly a tent that welcomes migrants from both Athens and Jerusalem.

This is a big tent that welcomes theological pluralism. That constitution was adopted on July 4, 1961. The merger that created the United Church of Christ was approved on June 25, 1957. In 1956 the two predecessor denominations reported a combined total of 2,185,000 members in 8,200 congregations. Back in 1956 the Congregational Christian Church, the larger partner in this merger, included 1.4 million members in 5,500 congregations.[5] At the end of 2000 the United Church of Christ included 1,377,320 members in 5,923 congregations, down from 1,841,312 members in 6,581 congregations in 1974.

One reason for this side trip, the first of several to be offered in this book, is that some readers may prefer the Athens and Jerusalem designations for the two parties rather than "progressive" and "conservative." A second reason is that the criteria for institutional and professional evaluation that the migrants from Athens brought to higher education have become embedded in the culture of The United Methodist Church. That long list includes a high value on academic credentials; a heavy emphasis on inputs into the system (academic degrees, financial subsidies, a reluctance to charge full cost user fees, apportionments, the promise of retirement benefits for the clergy, financial compensation for staff, real estate, sabbaticals for the professionals, a growing reliance on dollars rather than the transformation of lives as a basis for measuring performance, the creation of endowment funds to finance an uncertain future, and placing a high priority on guaranteed employment for adults); deference toward adults with impressive titles; hostility toward those who suggest the time has come to improve the efficiency of the system; hostility toward labor unions for employees; and a drift toward redefining what originally was a vocation or calling into a profession.

A third, and perhaps the most important reason for this side trip has been described by Professor James Turner.[6] Turner's thesis is that up "until the middle of the nineteenth century atheism and agnosticism were viewed in Western Society as bizarre aberrations." Turner contends that religious leaders pioneered the cultural acceptance of what he calls unbelief. While Turner does not use this terminology, he makes it clear that residents of Athens led this effort to make belief in God something between an irrelevant and superfluous concept. The residents of Jerusalem failed to win that contest.

Finally, a fourth reason is internal quarreling in the academy clearly is on the rise, paralleling the fact that never before in the brief history of The United Methodist Church have so many members of this denomination openly declared their ideological citizenship was in either Jerusalem or Athens.

Incidentally, contemporary demands for full disclosure require two statements. First, while my head was educated in Athens (or more precisely, at the University of Wisconsin in Madison 1941–42 and 1946–56), my heart was warmed in Jerusalem (or more precisely in the former Methodist Church). Second, I am only one of scores of writers who have committed to paper their worries about the future of our beloved denomination.[7] In reviewing my earlier writings I now must confess to a major mistake in my analysis.[8] I attributed the growing problems facing this denomination to an *unwillingness* to change. It took a long time, but finally I have realized that was an error. The heart of this issue may be an institutional *inability* to adapt to a changing economy and culture. That explains why the word *dysfunctional* appears so often in this book.

We now can move this discussion over to that second line in the sand, the battle over control of the denominational decision-making processes. Back in the 1940s and 1950s, there was a national consensus in America about American foreign policy. "Partisanship in foreign policy stops at the waters' edge" was the politically correct stance. In recent years that guiding generalization has been amended. Political control of national elective offices has moved ahead of foreign policy in both political parties. The current guiding principle is, "Partisanship in foreign policy is one road to winning national elections and the control of Congress." In a similar manner, partisan politics has changed the nature of the games played in the church. When the name of the game is control, partisan church politics become more highly visible.[9]

That game called "The Battle Over the Interpretation of Scripture" rarely attracts as many players or spectators as the game called "The Battle Over Control of Our Denomination." In recent decades one or both of these two games have been played in the Lutheran Church–Missouri Synod, the Episcopal Church USA, the Evangelical Lutheran Church in America, and the Southern Baptist Convention. The vast majority of the people in the pews would prefer to play a game called "Ministry, Missions, and Evangelism," but who listens to them?

Why should you read @ *Risk?*

One reason the book is so important is because it is designed to enlist more players to join in playing that game over control. One of the games in that never-ending series of contests was played in most annual conferences in 2003 in the selection of delegates to General Conferences. Another game will be played at the General Conference in 2004 when a national denominational budget for apportionments is adopted. The recommended total calls for an increase of something over $40 million in apportionments for the quadrennium. Approximately $18 million will be allocated for a 22 percent increase in the Episcopal Fund, along with a decrease of five in the number of active bishops in the jurisdictional conferences. The World Service Fund, frequently identified as a synonym for "missions," is budgeted for an increase of 6.5 percent, also of $18 million.

It also is important to note that the game over control is played following a different rulebook than is used to play the game about biblical interpretation. One big difference is that the losers in the game over Scripture frequently leave the playing field with a "live and let live" attitude about the future. It is not unusual, however, for the losers in that game over control to pick up their equipment, depart, and look for a playing field designed for that game called "Ministry, Missions, and Evangelism" where "Fulfilling the Great Commission" is the title on the cover of the rulebook.

Second, and perhaps most important of all, @ *Risk* caused this reader to ask a truly threatening question. Have the stresses and strains created by these quarrels over biblical interpretation and control torn so many holes in that Methodist wineskin (sometimes referred to as the constitution of The United Methodist Church) that it is beyond repair? Has the time come to discard that old wineskin and replace it with one or more new wineskins?

In other words, whether you are interested in participating in or watching either the game over biblical interpretation or the game over control, @ *Risk* is a book that should be on your reading list. To be more specific, @ *Risk* lifts up both the issue of biblical interpretation and also the issue of control. If you are ready to choose sides in this quarrel, @ *Risk* provides the perspective for one of those two sides.

Third, it focuses attention on the growing number and variety of renewal movements, caucuses, interest groups, parachurch organizations, protest groups, and publications that are influencing the decision-making processes in this denomination. While the list is far from complete and contains a few inaccuracies, the influence of these groups on both sides of this quarrel must be recognized.

Fourth, the book does draw clear lines in the sand. One difference I have is the number and variety of those lines in the sand are far greater than a reading of @ *Risk* suggests (see chapter 2).

Fifth, while it is not a central theme of @ *Risk,* this book does support my contention that the rise of individualism in the American culture is a clear threat to hierarchical structures as well as to elected representative government with constitutional limitations.

Finally, a section contributed by the Reverend Scott Campbell makes it clear that this is more than a family quarrel that can be resolved by serious dialogue among all parties. This is not simply a quarrel over the interpretation of Scripture. This is a constitutional crisis! The only way this quarrel can be resolved is by amending the constitution of The United Methodist Church. One possibility is the constitutional provision that states that the first and second Restrictive Rules can be amended by a "three-fourths majority of all the members of the Annual Conferences present and voting." That does open the door to changes in both doctrine and polity. It is unlikely, however, that any reader born before 1998 will live long enough to see a 75 percent majority support any radical change unless either one party or the other is able to control the selection of delegates from all but one or two annual conferences. The other alternative would be to dissolve the present denomination and create a successor denomination without the Restrictive Rules. That process almost certainly would require opening the door for any congregation to withdraw and retain title to its property after leaving.

Why Write This Book?

Why should a few dozen innocent trees be sacrificed to turn this manuscript into a book? One reason is a conviction that The United Methodist Church is being polarized by not simply two but at least two or three dozen lines in the sand. A second reason is, I do not see any easy resolution on the horizon. Many different games are being played, such as "Increasing the Retirement Benefits for Middle-aged Clergy."

As was pointed out earlier, each game attracts a different crowd of players and spectators than are attracted to most of the other games, and each has its own distinctive rulebook. Chess and tackle football are both games played by teenagers. Relatively few teenagers, however, play both games. Relatively few adults enjoy watching both. Each game has its own rulebook and the outcomes are different.

The outcome of two games currently being played in annual conferences all across this denomination will have a tremendous impact on the future of this branch of American Methodism. One game is called "Let's Reach, Attract, Serve, Nurture, Challenge, and Equip Generations Born After 1960 with the Gospel of Jesus Christ." A larger number of conferences have been engaged for three decades or longer in a game called "Let's Cut Back on the Number of Congregations and Members." These two games utilize radically different rulebooks and implement two different sets of operational policies. The future of this denomination will be heavily influenced by which becomes the more popular game in the early years of the twenty-first century.

One of the primary motivations for writing this book is a conviction the time has come to focus on a resolution of this contagious disease called intradenominational quarreling. The day has arrived to move from diagnosis, the focus of chapters 1 and 2 of this book, to searching for areas of agreement on both the definition of contemporary reality as well as on the diagnosis. That is the theme of chapter 3. Concurrently, anyone engaged in seeking a resolution of the current conflict will benefit from hearing a variety of perspectives. The book @ *Risk* provides one perspective. Chapter 4 opens the door to a half dozen different perspectives to be heard.

Perhaps the most difficult step in that process will be to gain agreement on what are the non-negotiable issues. Chapter 5 introduces that stage of the discussion. Chapter 6 invites those readers who want to eavesdrop on a few contemporary discussions about how to design ministries for the early years of the third millennium. That brief tour may be useful in evaluating a dozen possible scenarios plus a potential compromise for this denomination in the twenty-first century. That is the point of the final chapter and a big reason for writing this book.

WARNING! The lines in the sand may be so numerous and so deep that none of those scenarios could win the support of even 51 percent of the delegates to General Conference. It is easier to identify the symptoms of a failing institution than it is to win agreement for the complete diagnosis. Far more difficult, however, is gaining agreement for the appropriate prescription or therapy.

For example, what do you believe is the most accurate diagnostic statement? The central issue is the quarrel between the migrants from Jerusalem and those from Athens? Or do you believe the heart of the problem is the battle over control? Or do you believe a shrinking constituency and internal conflict are simply predictable "age-related" problems in an aging institution with an obsolete organizational structure? Or do you agree that an addiction to intradenominational quarreling tends to be self-perpetuating and eventually will naturally lead to schism? Or are you convinced that intradenominational quarreling is a contagious virus, and the top priority is to find a cure for that virus? Or do you agree with this author that (1) during the past hundred years this branch of American Methodism has evolved from what once was a covenant community organized around the unifying goal of spreading scriptural holiness[10] across the land into what today closely resembles a voluntary association of congregations and annual conferences, and (2) the system of governance that is appropriate for a covenant community will be somewhere between ineffective and counterproductive when utilized in a voluntary association that is not organized around a unifying goal? The next three chapters are designed to help inform your efforts to arrive at an accurate diagnosis.

CHAPTER ONE

THE MELTING OF OUR ICE CUBE

I magine a huge outdoor park with an open arena in the middle covered with sawdust. (Why sawdust? Because for a long period in American history sawdust was used in the storage of ice after it had been harvested for later use.)

Scattered across that sawdust are close to 1,200 ice cubes ranging in size from tiny to twelve feet in height. They are located here because the air temperature is a constant 28°F twenty-four hours a day, seven days a week. Each ice cube represents one of the approximately 1,200 denominations, religious bodies, associations, conventions, fellowships, and unions under that broad umbrella called organized religion in America. I have had the opportunity to meet with congregational leaders from slightly over one hundred of the larger religious bodies on their turf and on their agendas, but I have had no firsthand contact with members from most of them.

To the right is the second largest of these ice cubes. It represents the 16 million members in the Southern Baptist Convention who are scattered among nearly 42,000 congregations in the United States. (It should be noted that it is not unusual for the name of a Southern Baptist to be reported concurrently on the membership rolls of two or more SBC congregations.) Next to it is an ice cube about four times as large representing the 64 million baptized members carried on the membership rolls of the nearly 20,000 Roman Catholic parishes in America.

Over to the far left is the ice cube representing the Unitarian Universalist Association. This is an association of autonomous congregations formed in 1961 when two small bodies came together. This is a theologically liberal body that has grown from 192,000 in 946 congregations in 1974 to 220,000 in nearly 1,100 congregations at the end of 2002.

A little to the left of center is the third largest ice cube in this outdoor arena. It represents The United Methodist Church, with nearly 9.6 million lay, ordained, and preparatory members in slightly over 35,000 congregations. This ice cube is the product of several schisms and mergers over the past two hundred years.

The most recent of these institutional changes came in 1968 with the merger of The Methodist Church and the Evangelical United Brethren Church (EUB). In 1965 The Methodist Church reported a total of nearly 12.1 million (full plus preparatory) members in 38,876 congregations. The EUB Church reported a total of 840,000 members (resident plus nonresident, plus children) in 4,200 congregations in 1965. That came to a combined total of more than 13 million members in more than 43,000 congregations. Four years after that merger, at the end of 1972, The United Methodist Church reported 12.1 million (full plus preparatory) members in 39,626 congregations in the United States. By the end of 1977, nine years after that merger, that now-merged ice cube, with slightly over 11 million members (full plus preparatory) and 38,682 congregations, was smaller than The Methodist Church ice cube of 1965. Adding more ice may not increase the size of the ice cube!

Nearby are three other relatively very large ice cubes. To the left is the ice cube representing the United Church of Christ (UCC). It is the product of mergers that occurred in 1931, 1934, and 1957. At the end of 2000, the UCC reported 1.4 million confirmed members in 5,923 congregations, down from slightly over 1.8 million members in 6,581 congregations in 1974. To the right of that ice cube is the one representing the Evangelical Lutheran Church in America, with 5.1 million baptized members in 10,700 parishes. Between those two is the ice cube representing the Presbyterian Church (U.S.A.), with nearly 3.5 million baptized members in 11,000 congregations. All three of these ice cubes share three common characteristics: (1) each is the product of several mergers, (2) each one is larger than 97 percent of the ice cubes in this area, and (3) each one has been melting in recent years.

One lesson from this brief visit to four of the largest ice cubes in this arena is that adding fresh water, in the form of new generations of churchgoers, may be a more productive way to increase the size than adding old ice in the form of a merger to an existing ice cube.

A Long-term Perspective

For those who prefer to review history rather than study aging ice cubes, a useful indicator is the changing proportion of the American population who are members of The United Methodist Church. For close to a century this branch of American Methodism or its predecessor denominations counted 1 out of every 15 to 18 Americans as a baptized member. That ratio now stands at about 1 out of 30. A ratio of 1 to 30 would require a combined (lay, ordained, and preparatory) membership of 10 million when the American population passes 300 million in the year 2007. At the end of 2000 that combined total was 9.7 million, down from a combined total of 12.2 million back in 1964. To return to that 1 in 15 ratio of 1965 by 2007, when the population of the United States is projected to pass 300 million, would require more than doubling the current membership by 2007. That is an unlikely possibility.

(For those readers who want to compare apples with apples, and oranges with oranges, in 1965 the former Methodist Church reported a total of 10,331,574 confirmed members, a number equal to 5.32 percent of the total American population. At the end of 2001, The United Methodist Church reported a total of 8,249,597 confirmed members, a number equal to 2.89 percent of the

Table A RATIO OF MEMBERSHIP TO POPULATION[1] The United Methodist Church and Its Predecessor Denominations	
Year	Proportion
1771	1 in 2,050 Americans
1816	1 in 39 Americans
1890	1 in 16 Americans
1906	1 in 18 Americans
1916	1 in 15 Americans
1926	1 in 16 Americans
1960	1 in 15 Americans
1965	1 in 15 Americans
1970	1 in 17 Americans
1980	1 in 21 Americans
1990	1 in 24 Americans
2000	1 in 29 Americans

American population. The *big* increase was in the number of retired clergy from 6,042 in The Methodist Church plus 720 in the EUB Church in 1965 to 14,995 at the end of 2001.)

While the ratio of membership to population is a useful historical indicator, several others are more revealing as diagnostic tools.

What Are the Best Indicators?

Recently, in discussing with a group of congregational leaders this melting of the United Methodist ice cube, I referred to a dozen reasonably objective criteria.

The first calls for a global perspective. In 1972 The United Methodist Church reported a total of 12,543,000 members. The overwhelming majority of these, 12,067,000, were members of

American congregations. The remaining 476,000, or 3.8 percent, were members of churches affiliated with the Central Conferences in other parts of the world. (These totals include both full members and preparatory members.) At the end of 2001 the equivalent statistics were 9,591,000 members in America and 2,466,000 in the Central Conferences for a grand total of 12,057,000, with Central Conferences accounting for slightly over 20 percent of the grand total. (In chapter 3 I will explain why these may be the most significant pairs of numbers in this book.)

"How come our membership is increasing overseas and decreasing here?" inquired one layperson. "I don't know all the reasons," I replied, "but certainly high on that list of variables is the Central Conferences sharply increased the number of congregations from 4,691 in 1972 to 6,920 at the end of 2001. Here in the United States we reduced the number of congregations from 39,626 in 1972 to 35,275 at the end of 2001."

Next we discussed what I believe to be the most sensitive indicator. One way to measure the current attractiveness of any congregation in America today is to compare the number of new members received during the past year or two or three with earlier years. That same criterion can be applied to denominations. The two predecessor denominations reported a combined total of slightly over 816,000 new members received in 1956. Eight years later that total had dropped to 730,000. Four years after the merger, this new denomination reported a total of slightly over 500,000 new members received in 1972. For 1980 that figure was 420,000, and in 2000 it was down to 398,000, less than one-half the 1956 total.

One explanation is the increase in the competition among the churches in American Protestantism for future constituents raised the bar. To attract the generations born after 1960, congregations had the choice between raising the quality of what they offered or welcoming fewer newcomers who chose them as their new church home. A second explanation introduces two other indicators.

What proportion of the current congregations in a denominational family have been meeting at the same address for more than forty years? The higher that proportion, the more likely that denomination will be shrinking in the number of constituents. In 1906, for example, more than 40 percent of the congregations affiliated with the Methodist Episcopal Church or the Methodist Episcopal Church South had been organized during the past thirty-seven years. Approximately 7 percent of the 35,000 congregations in The United Methodist Church today have been organized during the past thirty-seven years. In other words, aging institutions tend to have difficulty attracting younger generations.

A fourth and related indicator is the number of new congregations organized each year. The basic guideline is to remain on a plateau in size; a denomination should organize the number of new congregations each year that is equivalent to 1 percent of the total number of existing congregations. For the UMC 1 percent of 350,000 is 350. The actual number since 1965 has averaged out to fewer than 75 per year, so the ice cube continues to melt.

That introduces a fifth indicator. It is difficult to find a denomination in American Protestantism that has been able to both (1) decrease the number of congregations and (2) increase the number of constituents. One explanation is that American churchgoers searching for a new church home prefer to help pioneer the new rather than perpetuate the old.

A sixth indicator also is especially relevant to congregational life. A useful diagnostic question is to look at that list of members who left that congregation during the past twenty-four months. Let us assume that two congregations meeting in buildings in the same community each report 40 removals from the membership roster during the past twenty-four months. In one, 30 of those 40 left to join another congregation in that same community, 5 died, and 5 moved out of town. In the other congregation, 22 of the 40 died, 1 left for another church in town, and 17 moved away. A second look revealed that first congregation had been split following the arrival of the new pastor, while the second church was an aging congregation, and 14 of the 17 who moved away had moved to the Sunbelt to retire. In short, the higher the death rate, the more likely that ice cube will be melting.

The annual death rate for the American population, age 14 and over, climbed from 11.8 per 1,000 in 1952 to 12.2 per 1,000 in 1970. Thanks to remarkable discoveries in medical science, early detection, better highways, safer cars, and the reduction in the use of tobacco, that annual death rate dropped from 12.2 persons, age 14 and over, in 1970 to 10.5 in 2002. One consequence is an increase in the number of Protestant church members in America who are age 65 and older. They have chosen to go to church rather than to the cemetery.

The annual death rate in the former Methodist Church dropped from 8.9 per 1,000 full (confirmed) members in 1952 to 7.4 in 1964. For the former EUB Church that annual death rate increased from 10.7 in 1952 to 12 in 1966. The annual death rate among full members in the UMC rose from 10.4 per 1,000 in 1970 to 12.6 in 1980 to 14.5 per 1,000 full members in 2001. Mature readers may be interested to note that the annual death rate for all American males age 65 to 74 dropped from 12,126 per 100,000 in that age cohort in 1940 to 8,817 in 1980 to 6,863 in 2000. For American females age 65 to 74 the annual death rate plunged from 10,369 per 100,000 in 1940 to 5,440 in 1980 to 4,923 in 2000. For those age 75 and over the annual death rate per 100,000 dropped by approximately one-third between 1940 and 2000. Those trends help to explain why that UMC ice cube is melting more slowly than if the life-expectancy rates for mature Americans had not been extended.

One of the most sensitive indicators is the average attendance at the corporate worship of God. This tends to be a more uniform criterion than membership because of the huge variations in defining who is a member. Back in 1965, the first year the Methodist Church asked congregations to report their average worship attendance, that number was something over 3.9 million. (We do not have a more precise number because hundreds of congregations did not report their average worship attendance that year.) Add 405,000 for EUB worship attendance, and the combined total exceeded 4.3 million. In 1972 that indicator was 3.7 million, and for 1980 it was slightly under 3.6 million. By 1990 that sharp decline had begun to level off, and worship attendance averaged 3.47 million for that year. The 1990s confirmed the plateau as that indicator was in the 3.47 million to 3.55 million range year after year. That decrease of 20 percent over a quarter of a century had been turned into a plateau. At the end of 2001 the average worship attendance in this new denomination was only 10 percent less than it had been in the former Methodist Church in 1965. Has the ice cube stopped melting?

A closer look at the statistics on average worship attendance, however, reveal one reason not to be overly complacent. If we carefully select 1,000 of those 35,000 organized United Methodist congregations in existence at the end of 2000, one hundred of whom were organized after 1990, and identify them as Group A and identify the remaining 34,000 as Group B, what do we have?

First of all, we discover that an unknown number of the people who were members of one of the 2,500 UM congregations that dissolved or was merged into another church during the 1991–2000 decade are now worshiping with a UM church in Group B, while others are worshiping with a church in Group A.

Second, during that 1991–2000 decade the 1,000 congregations in Group A reported a combined increase in their average worship attendance of more than 400,000. The 34,000 UM churches in Group B reported a combined net decrease of at least 400,000 in their average attendance, despite the fact that several thousand reported a modest increase during that decade.

Most of our UM ice cube continues to shrink under the sun of increased competition for new constituents, but it remains about the same size overall as fresh water is sprayed on one narrow section of our beloved ice cube.

A more comprehensive analysis covering a shorter time frame was completed by a UM layman, Richard P. Deitzler, and published in May 2001.[2] This analysis traced the reported average worship attendance of 34,670 UM congregations from 1994 to

the end of 1999. These data were reported for each annual conference, and the congregations were grouped by average worship
attendance.

In the Oklahoma Conference, for example, 9 of the 14 congregations averaging 500 or more at worship in 1994 reported an
increase in attendance over the next five years, while 149 of 226
averaging fewer than 50 at worship in 1994 reported a loss in
attendance over the next five years. In the West Ohio
Conference 73 of the 113 congregations reporting an average
worship attendance of 250 or more experienced an increase,
while 522 of the 847 averaging fewer than 100 at worship
reported a decrease.

For the denomination as a whole 76 percent of the congregations reporting an average worship attendance of 500 or more in
1994 reported an increase, as did 65 percent of those averaging
250 to 499 at worship and 55 percent of those averaging 150 to
249 at worship. Only 49 percent of those averaging 100 to 149 at
worship reported an increase, but that was a better record than
those averaging fewer than 100 at worship. While they
accounted for 72 percent of all UM congregations, only 40 percent of these small congregations reported an increase in their
attendance during that five-year period.

Whether it was intentional or not cannot be determined, but
in at least three dozen annual conferences the operational policies in effect during the past four decades have produced an
increase in the number of small congregations and a decrease in
the number averaging 500 or more at worship. This analysis by
Richard Deitzler suggests those operational policies have been an
influential factor in the shrinking of that UM ice cube. That also
is one reason why some readers will place trends in average worship attendance close to the top of this list of useful indicators in
the annual performance audit of a congregation or district or
annual conference.

This long discussion on average worship attendance introduces
an eighth criterion. What is the design used in planting new missions? A common design in the third quarter of the twentieth
century was to appoint and subsidize a pastor to go out and

launch a new mission in a geographically defined area. That design usually produced one of three outcomes. The most common was a new congregation that plateaued UM an average worship attendance of fewer than 150. The second most common was a new mission that disappeared from view before its tenth birthday. The rarest was a congregation that by the end of year five was averaging at least 350 at worship.

In recent years a more common design in American Protestantism has been to assemble a team of two or three full-time program people, plus two to five part-time or volunteer specialists. The focus is not on where prospective future constituents reside, but rather on their common demographic characteristics and/or where they are on their own personal spiritual journey. Instead of planning to organize a new neighborhood congregation for people who prefer to walk to church, this model calls for launching a large regional church for people who are comfortable driving to work, to shops, to entertainment and recreational experiences, and to church. A typical goal is an average worship attendance of at least 350 by the end of the first month, and financially fully self-supporting by one year after that first public worship service. In other words, an eighth indicator can be stated as a question: In planting new missions does your annual conference use a model designed to produce small congregations or large ones?

A ninth indicator is given a very high priority in several denominational traditions. What is the denomination-wide trend in baptisms? In 1956, when the number of live births reported in the United States was 4.2 million, the Methodist Church reported a total of 408,460 baptisms for all ages. Add 30,000 for the EUB Church.

In 1990, when the number of babies born in the United States was slightly under 4.2 million, The United Methodist Church reported a total of 179,223 baptisms for people of all ages. In 2001, when the number of births was 3.8 million, the number of baptisms had dropped to 151,720. This indicator may not be as significant as it first appears, because most UM pastors will affirm the baptism of a person who was baptized in any other Christian tradition. Therefore, a more useful but rarely used indicator is the number of preparatory members. In 1965 the Methodist Church reported 1,822,198. Add 8,000 children under age 13 in the EUB Church, and the total was approximately 1,830,000. In 1972 that number was 1,732,000—down nearly 100,000. Eighteen years later in 1990, the number of preparatory members had dropped to 1,647,000, and at the end of 2001 that indicator stood at 1,292,666.

How should that decrease be interpreted? Is it simply a product of an aging constituency? Or primarily a result of fewer full members? Or a consequence of that long-term cutback in new church development? Or to the trend toward smaller families? Or simply as a predictable consequence of the melting of that ice cube?

At that point an impatient pragmatist interrupted, "According to my count you've described ten indicators to evaluate how we're doing as a denomination, and you still haven't said a word about money! That may not be one of your indicators, but I believe it belongs among the top three or four. In my annual conference every district superintendent sends a monthly mailing to every congregation reporting what their total apportionment is for the year, the amount received to date, and the percentage paid. I know other conferences send those reports quarterly, but I've never heard of a conference or district sending out monthly or quarterly performance reports to each church on their average worship attendance or new members received or preparatory membership or baptisms or death rates. Is the money coming in or not?"

"Patience!" I urged this impatient learner. "We'll come to that in a few minutes, but I placed it last of these twelve for three reasons. First, the church is in the ministry business, not the money business. Money is a means to an end, so we need to keep it in perspective. That's why it's last on this agenda. Second, money is not a big issue in Methodism. If it were, this denomination would have created a United Methodist Foundation in 1968 or 1972 rather than waiting until the end of the biggest economic boom in American history to create it.[3] If it had been created as a part of the merger of 1968, it could have accumulated at least $300 million in foundation-owned assets by 2000. That could have yielded $15 million in matching grants to conferences for new church development. At $100,000 per grant, that would help finance 150 new missions annually."

"That's not the reason for the delay in authorizing the creation of the foundation," corrected a person who had been a delegate to General Conference in 1992 and 1996. "The reason it wasn't launched earlier is because when it comes to decision making, we have a dysfunctional system."

"A third reason why I don't believe this denomination feels a need for more money," I continued, "is the eight-year limitation on the tenure of a bishop in any one episcopal area. In other traditions with a long history of the episcopacy, a common responsibility of a bishop is to raise money from wealthy members. That usually requires cultivating long-term relationships with potential contributors. A bishop might raise a million or two in that first quadrennium, and a few million more in the second, but the big payout probably won't come until years seven or eight to twenty of that relationship."

"Where would those big contributions go?" inquired another person. "To the conference budget?"

"Possibly," I explained, "but more likely they would be designated for a special purpose such as new church development or ministerial education or the revitalization of inner-city ministries or to fund the pension system or for capital improvements or a camp or for children's ministries or to fund new ministries. The bequests usually are directed to the conference foundation."

"What's number eleven on your list?" asked someone who wanted to return to the agenda.

This next-to-last indicator was referred to back in the discussion about the research completed by Richard P. Deitzler. During the 1994–99 era the congregations most likely to report an increase in their average worship attendance were the churches averaging 500 or more at worship in 1994.

That parallels one of the most highly visible patterns in American life during the last third of the twentieth century. "They are bigger than they used to be." The word *they* in that sentence applies to professional football players, bookstores, teenagers, pickup trucks, airport terminals, shoes, grocery stores, farms, hospitals, stomachs, bathrooms, parking lots, banks, universities, cows, medical clinics, motion picture theaters, single family detached homes, public high schools, commercial aircraft, lawn mowers, foundations, the federal government, coffee cups, tractors, driveways, T-shirts, soft drink bottles, paper clips, dump trucks, corridors, public libraries, closets, television sets, garages, and Protestant churches.

That generalization also applies to United Methodist, Southern Baptist, and independent Protestant congregations in the South. It also

Table B						
NUMBER OF LARGE UNITED METHODIST CONGREGATIONS						
Average Worship Attendance of 500 or More						
By Jurisdictions						
YEAR	NE	NC	SC	SE	W	TOTAL
1965*	109	196	161	193	104	763
1980	31	97	129	178	40	475
2001	60	122	209	361	52	804

*The totals for 1965 include five large congregations in the Central Jurisdiction. These have been included in the appropriate geographical jurisdiction for the 1965 figures in this table. The 1965 numbers are for the former Methodist Church and do NOT include the large EUB congregations of 1965.

applies to black churches all across the country and to nondenominational congregations in the North and West. With a couple of exceptions, that generalization does not apply to the United Methodist conferences in the North and West.

Between 1965 and 2001 the population of the United States increased by approximately 45 percent. The number of Protestant congregations averaging 500 or more at worship at least doubled and probably tripled during those thirty-six years. Should that number 804 representing the number of large UM congregations at the end of 2001 be compared with the 475 at the end of 1980, or the 763 of 1965 (plus the number of large EUB churches in 1965)? Or, should it be compared with a "keeping up with the population growth of 1965 to 2001" of slightly over 1,100? Or, should it be compared with the pattern in the rest of American Protestantism and a number somewhere between 1,600 and 2,300?

Two reasons can be offered to explain why this trend is being described here. One is the wealth of evidence that reveals American Protestant churchgoers born after 1960 can be found in disproportionately large numbers in congregations founded after 1960 and/or congregations that average more than 500 at worship.

The second reason is that back in 1965 the three northern and western jurisdictions accounted for 54 percent of all the large Methodist congregations in the United States. By the end of 2001 that proportion had plunged to 29 percent. If those three jurisdictions had increased the number of large churches at the same rate as in the two southern jurisdictions (61 percent), the grand total at the end of 2001 would have been 1,228 congregations averaging 500 or more.

Does the sun of competition shine hotter on United Methodism in the North than in the South? Or, is that trend a consequence of the operational policies followed in the North?

One reason to place money as the last of these twelve indicators is it should be seen as a means to an end. A second is the absence of widely agreed upon criteria for evaluation. Should the increase in giving be compared to the increase in the consumer price index? Or to the increase in per capita personal income? Or to the increase in governmental expenditures? Or to what a full tithe would yield?

A third reason is that large congregations tend to be the "cash cows" for annual conferences. They send the conference far more money than they receive back in services. One consequence is the second most effective tactic to fund the conference budget is to increase the number of very large congregations. The most effective tactic is to strengthen the ties of denominational loyalty. The third was mentioned earlier, the giving circles created by the bishop to fund special needs.[4]

In 1960 Methodist congregations reported slightly under $540 million in receipts, of which $80 million (14.8 percent) was allocated for benevolences. Add $52 million, including nearly $9 million for benevolences in the EUB churches, and the grand total was $592 million. Between 1960 and 2000 the Consumer Price Index climbed from 29.6 (1982–84 = 100) to 183. Thus we multiply $592 by 6.18 to allow for the impact of inflation, or $3.658 billion. If we multiply that combined total of $89 million for benevolences by 6.18, the result is $550 million after allowing for inflation.

What were the reported totals for 2000? Total receipts were $4.76 billion, with $491 million for benevolences or 10.3 percent of that grand total. Why did giving for benevolences not rise as fast as the increase in total giving? That question opens the door to speculation. Most pastors probably will agree it did; but as the competition for the charitable dollar became more intense, more of the laity allocated a larger proportion of their charitable contributions to colleges, universities, theological schools, independent missionary-sending organizations, parachurch organizations, and a huge variety of attractive causes such as housing the homeless, feeding the hungry, and community ministries.

Another explanation is "naturally." That decrease in the number of congregations, the number of members, and the number of worshipers naturally produced a decrease in the number of dollars received by congregations, or the number of discretionary dollars left over after paying the bills required to keep the church doors open.[5]

At this point the temperature of the discussion escalated as someone declared, "Your use of the inflationary factor is simply an attempt to paper over a crisis! A more realistic comparison begins with the fact that per capita personal income in the United States increased from $2,226 annually in 1960 to $29,676 in 2000. That's an increase of 13.3 times in forty years. We multiply that grand total of $592 million in 1960 by 13.3. That comes out to $7.9 billion. Next we subtract 23 percent to allow for that decrease in membership from 10.7 million confirmed members in 1960 to 8.34 million at the end of 2000. That means our congregations should have received approximately $6 billion in 2000. That's a whole lot more than the actual $4.76 billion that was received. How do you explain that gap of well over $1 billion? If the giving had kept up with the increase in the average per capita personal income, our congregations would have received $1.25 for every dollar that actually was contributed."

"One reason may be that we have more members who are retired and living on a fixed income," suggested an elderly participant.

"If you ask me, I believe we have overlooked two of the most influential factors," commented the senior minister of a congregation averaging about 450 at worship. "For years we depended on that big group of midsized congregations averaging between 100 and 349 at worship to carry a large share of the load for paying apportionments in full. Back in 1972 we had more than 10,400 congregations in that size bracket. At the end of 2001 that number was down to fewer than 8,300. While we reduced the number of midsized churches by 20 percent, we have increased the number averaging fewer than 35 at worship by over a thousand from 9,631 in 1972 to 10,541 in 2001. If you use worship attendance to calculate the average contribution per capita, as a general rule the per average worship attendance giving is much higher in our midsized and large churches than it is in small congregations. Likewise, the average payment to apportionments is higher as the size of the congregation increases. Combine those two factors and that will explain a big chunk of that billion-dollar gap."

"Let's back up and talk about how much our congregations should allocate to fund the budgets of our conference and national agencies," urged a young layperson. "Recently, our pastor told us that out of every dollar received by our congregations about 83 cents stays in the local church; nearly 13 cents goes to the districts, conferences, and jurisdictions, while only 4 cents, including the UMW (United Methodist Women) funds, goes to the national agencies. How do we compare with other churches on that one?"

"Someone needs to take a second look at that 13 percent figure," challenged a layperson who is an expert on budgeting. "A number of annual conferences, including mine, use apportionment dollars to partially subsidize health insurance premiums or pension payments for pastors. That means a congregation may pay $15,000 in apportionments but get part of that back in subsidies. My hunch is those numbers probably are closer to 88, 8, and 4."

"To get back to the question on how we compare with other denominations, that will depend on your choice of a reference point," I suggested. "At one end of this spectrum we have the independent churches that do not send any money to denominational headquarters since they don't carry a denominational affiliation. Not too far this side of them is the United Church of Christ. They reported recently that out of every dollar received by a congregation, the conferences collect about 2 1/2 cents, the national offices' and special offering account for 2 cents, and the churches retain 95 1/2 cents. They also report that after allowing for inflation, per-member contributions for their national agencies plunged from the equivalent of $4.92 in 1967 to $1.69 in 2001. If you translate that into United Methodist terms, that would mean an annual conference that included congregations with a combined total of 300,000 members would be sending $507,000 annually to the national agencies. Near the middle of that spectrum are the Roman Catholic parishes. The typical Catholic parish in the United States sends an amount equal to 4 to 8 percent of the parish receipts to headquarters. Frequently the diocese will allocate some of those dollars to subsidize parochial schools in low-income parishes.

"Over on the more generous side of this spectrum is the Southern Baptist Convention. Founded in 1845 as a voluntary association of autonomous congregations, for the next one hundred thirty years the SBC was organized around two rallying points—missions and evangelism. In recent decades that has been enlarged to a half-dozen rallying points, missions, and evangelism, expanding from a regional constituency to a North American religious body, reaching members of ethnic minority groups in North America, intradenominational quarreling, and regional autonomy. In 1987, SBC congregations in the United States contributed an overall average of 10.5 percent of their undesignated receipts, and 7.9 percent of their total receipts for all purposes to the Cooperative Program, the equivalent of what United Methodists call apportionments. For 2002 those allocations had dropped to 7.4 percent and 5.3 percent respectively. In 2002, SBC congregations allocated 11 percent of their total receipts to all missional causes, down from 15 percent back in 1987. Three explanations for those decreases were the rising costs of health insurance for paid staff, the price tag on intradenominational quarreling, and the preference of a growing number of donors to contribute directly to a charitable cause with excellent accountability rather than to contribute through a bureaucratic structure.

"In the Episcopal Church USA, parishes typically are asked to send 10 percent of their total receipts to headquarters.

"At the most generous end of this spectrum are the Seventh-day Adventists. All members are expected to return to the Lord the first 10 percent of their income. That entire tithe goes to denominational treasuries. The largest single share is allocated to pay the compensation for all the ministers, including the parish pastors."

"How do the Seventh-day Adventist congregations pay their bills such as utilities, secretarial staff, and maintenance of the real estate?" asked a puzzled participant.

"Those expenditures, including building programs and other local expenses, are paid out of voluntary contributions over and above the tithes. When you hear the minister announce that the time in the worship service has come to receive your tithes, gifts, and offerings, that includes returning to the Lord his tithe plus your gifts in gratitude of the blessings you have received from God, and your offering to support the ministry of your congregation."

After a period of shocked silence, an elderly baseball fan changed the subject.

"You sure place a great reliance on statistics," he observed. "Have you been trained by Billy Beane, the general manager of the Oakland Athletics? He also depends on a statistical analysis in selecting players in the amateur draft and in making trades."[6]

"I've never met Billy Beane, but I began to suffer with that team when they were the Philadelphia A's, long before Beane was born," I replied. "You have raised a crucial point, but the parallel is not in the use of statistics. Traditionally, baseball scouts placed a high value on credentials such as age, athletic ability, speed, the ability to catch and throw a baseball, and batting averages. Beane came along a few years ago and began to emphasize performance, what I am describing as outcomes. He has revolutionized the criteria for evaluating baseball players. I want to emphasize outcomes in the church in terms of ministry, mission, and evangelism rather than continue to focus on inputs into the system such as money, academic degrees, appointments, salaries, apportionments, titles, and real estate. For example, when a pastor telephones me with a question, I often will inquire, 'What is your average worship attendance?' I never ask, 'How many academic degrees have you earned?' or 'How much money does your congregation send to headquarters?' I am more interested in outcomes than inputs, and many of these outcomes can be quantified."

Regional Differences

If our perspective is shifted from the historical rate of shrinkage in the UM ice cube to a regional view, several changes stand out. Table C reports the combined membership of the two predecessor denominations in the thirty states with the largest number of members in 1960, and the reported UM membership for 2000. Those changes can be compared with the change in the population of each of those thirty states between 1960 and 2000.

With one exception, the ten states with the largest number of members in 1960 also were the ten largest in 2000. The exception was Florida replaced Indiana.

Among the greatest changes in the rank order were Illinois slipped from fourth to tenth, North Carolina climbed from sixth to third, and Georgia moved up from ninth to fifth. On that list

Table C						
FORTY YEARS LATER						
CHANGES IN POPULATION AND IN MEMBERSHIP *OF UNITED METHODIST CHURCHES*						
THE 30 STATES WITH OVER 100,000 MEMBERS IN 1960						
Population (x 1,000)			UM Membership			
	1960	2000	Changes	1960[7]	2000[8]	Changes
Pennsylvania	11,319	12,281	8%	771,313	541,247	-30%
Texas	9,580	20,852	118%	764,587	801,952	+ 5%
Ohio	9,706	11,353	17%	748,706	454,994	-39%
Illinois	10,081	12,419	23%	532,708	293,861	-45%
New York	16,782	18,976	13%	485,320	326,537	-33%
North Carolina	4,573	8,049	76%	464,692	516,299	+11%
Indiana	4,662	6,080	30%	425,425	230,262	-46%
Virginia	3,967	7,079	78%	425,011	382,684	-10%
Georgia	3,943	8,186	108%	378,668	452,715	+19%
Tennessee	3,575	5,689	59%	376,901	319,264	-15%
California	15,717	33,872	116%	324,367	180,858	-42%
Alabama	3,274	4,447	36%	314,413	263,880	-16%
Iowa	2,758	2,926	6%	313,078	201,204	-36%
Michigan	7,823	9,938	27%	303,599	177,930	-41%
Missouri	4,320	5,595	29%	275,394	182,725	-33%

Table C (continued)						

FORTY YEARS LATER

CHANGES IN POPULATION AND IN MEMBERSHIP OF UNITED METHODIST CHURCHES

THE 30 STATES WITH OVER 100,000 MEMBERS IN 1960

	Population (x 1,000)			UM Membership		
	1960	2000	Changes	1960[7]	2000[8]	Changes
Florida	4,952	15,982	222%	270,236	378,522	+40%
Kansas	2,179	2,688	23%	267,305	165,166	-37%
Maryland	3,113	5,296	70%	256,755	239,093	-7%
Oklahoma	2,336	3,451	48%	252,929	259,258	+3%
West Virginia	1,860	1,808	-3%	252,020	125,336	-50%
South Carolina	2,392	4,012	68%	230,364	242,891	+5%
Mississippi	2,182	2,845	31%	220,228	190,395	-14%
Kentucky	3,041	4,042	33%	206,499	169,622	-18%
New Jersey	6,103	8,414	38%	192,601	112,484	-39%
Arkansas	1,789	2,673	49%	181,627	144,342	-21%
Wisconsin	3,953	5,364	35%	151,073	104,364	-31%
Nebraska	1,417	1,711	21%	140,970	94,398	-33%
Louisiana	3,260	4,469	37%	140,116	127,060	-9%
Minnesota	3,414	4,919	44%	136,839	94,798	-30%
Massachusetts	5,160	6,349	23%	100,823	52,106	-48%
U.S.A.	180,671	281,422	56%	10,665,000	8,326,616	-22%

Table D	
THE TEN LARGEST	
in UM Membership	
1960	2000
Pennsylvania	Texas
Texas	Pennsylvania
Ohio	North Carolina
Illinois	Ohio
New York	Georgia
North Carolina	Virginia
Indiana	Florida
Virginia	New York
Georgia	Tennessee
Tennessee	Illinois

Indiana slipped from seventh to fifteenth, while California dropped from eleventh to nineteenth.

Another notable change was that back in 1960 Pennsylvania membership was 1 percent larger than the membership in Texas; but by 2000 Texas included 48 percent more members than were found in the Pennsylvania churches.

Only six states out of these thirty (Texas, Florida, North Carolina, Georgia, Oklahoma, and South Carolina) reported a net increase in membership during those four decades. The greatest losses in actual numbers were in Ohio, Illinois, Pennsylvania, and Indiana. It is not a coincidence that those four states were at the geographical heart of the EUB Church. When that big fish set out to swallow that little fish back in 1968, a lot of minnows escaped, and the big fish was incapacitated for a long time with digestive problems. The combined net loss in membership in Ohio, Pennsylvania, and Illinois between 1960 and 2000 was slightly more than the membership of the EUB Church in America in 1966.

Six of the other twenty states (Alaska, Arizona, Delaware, Hawaii, Nevada, and Utah) reported an increase in UM membership during that forty-year period. The largest numerical increase was 7,084 in Arizona. The other fourteen, plus the District of Columbia, reported a decrease, with the largest numerical decreases in Oregon, Washington, the District of Columbia, and Colorado. In percentage terms, the decreases in membership in the District of Columbia, Oregon, New Mexico, and Montana, exceeded 40 percent.

In summary, the United Methodist retreat has been the most pronounced in the Northeast, the Midwest, and the West. In thirty-eight of the fifty states this branch of American Methodism reported a net decrease in membership between 1960 and 2000.

Why?

That last sentence evokes the question of why did this happen? One explanation was offered in the introduction. Systems produce what they are designed to produce, and the current UM system is designed to produce fewer congregations and fewer members.

Another explanation focuses on demographic changes. While the number of adults worshiping with a predominantly white Protestant congregation in the United States on the typical weekend increased by more than one-third between 1960 and 2000, the population cohorts are not the same. Approximately one-half of those 10.7 million members of the two predecessor denominations in 1960 died during the next four decades. In other words, the number-one explanation for that 22 percent decline in membership was death. The number-two reason was the failure to replace all of them. A reasonable estimate is more than 4 million of the persons on the membership rolls of UM congregations at the end of 2000 will die before 2040, and that number may be closer to 5 million.

A third subjective explanation for the numerical decline of several religious bodies in America since 1960 focuses on the term *institutional loyalty*.[9] The erosion of inherited institutional loyalties can be seen in both the Republican and Democratic political parties, among the customers of the United States Postal Service, in the enrollment decisions of high school seniors preparing for college, in the sales figures for motor vehicles, and in the marketing problems confronting the owners of famous brand names.

On the ecclesiastical scene it is most clearly visible in the efforts to finance denominational systems, both Protestant and Roman Catholic. In the 1950s, when someone pressed that button labeled denominational loyalty, it usually produced a flood of checks and paper money. When that button is pushed today, the message on the computer screen frequently reads, "That system is no longer operative." One example is this: in 1956 Methodist congregations reported receiving a combined total of 309,760 members by letters of transfer from other Methodist churches; in 2000 the equivalent number was 113,042.

From this traveler's perspective, one of the most influential factors has been the recent increase in the level of intradenominational quarreling.[10] Today's church shoppers tend to choose a new church home on the expectation it will nurture their spiritual growth, challenge them to become the person God intended them to be, and equip them to be engaged in doing ministry. Relatively few are looking for a church home where they will be challenged to either watch or participate in a divisive intradenominational quarrel.

Likewise in interviewing recent new members in numerically growing congregations, I usually begin with two questions: *What brought you here the first time? Why did you decide to join this congregation?* Rarely do I hear anyone explain, "When we moved here, we decided to look for a church that places a high priority on sending money to denominational headquarters, and this is the only one we found that needs people to help achieve that goal." One way to avoid either of these two scenarios is to choose a nondenominational congregation organized around helping pilgrims on a religious quest find meaning in life.

Another explanation is that it is difficult to find a Christian religious tradition in America that has been able to increase its constituency by closing more churches than it opens. The retreat from the large central cities and older suburbs in the North and West clearly has been a factor.

Another subjective explanation can be summarized in one word—*competition*. The competition for future constituents among grocery stores, private church-related, four-year liberal arts colleges; hotels and motels; commercial airlines; financial institutions; hospitals; motion picture theaters; and Protestant congregations is far more intense today than it was in 1960.

One of the consequences is the bar has been raised in the evaluation of performance. It is far more difficult to be an effective parish pastor today than it was in the 1960s. The expectations people bring to church are both greater in number and variety as well as more difficult to meet. A simple example is, the members of the neighborhood congregation of 1960 usually chose from among two or three hospitals when that need arose, and the clergy usually were accorded deferential treatment. Today the members of that large regional church may choose from among six to ten hospitals, and recent federal legislation makes the pastor appear to be an uninvited intruder rather than a welcome ally. Additional examples include communication skills, youth ministries, administration, marriage, weekday programming, leadership, conflict resolution, and learning groups.

Likewise the district superintendent is expected to bring a far higher level of competence than was required as recently as the 1970s in such areas of expertise as litigation; ecumenism; building design; land use controls; the design of customized ministry plans; that shift from producer-driven Christian education to consumer-driven learning opportunities; staffing configurations for very large congregations; world missions; new church development; the issues involved in succession when that long-tenured senior minister departs; community ministries; evangelism; fund-raising; congregational governance; and, most important of all, the mobilization and utilization of human resources.

This is especially difficult when the same district may include four Latino congregations; two megachurches with each averaging over 1,500 at worship; twelve congregations, each served by a licensed lay minister and the largest averaging 45 at worship; two Korean congregations, one downtown church that is now less than half the size it was in 1955; two new suburban missions; five ex-neighborhood congregations that have been drifting down the road to oblivion; a new African mission; a rural congregation founded in 1885 that is now in the middle of one of the fastest growing communities in the state; one Chinese congregation; a midsized congregation in which the two elders are both personally and professionally incompatible; three African American congregations and two self-identified black churches; four two-point rural circuits; and one university church.

In 1966 one district superintendent told me, "It took me two years to learn the job, and I now have four years left to do the job." Today, a reasonable expectation is a new district superintendent who is a lifelong learner and, depending on the mix of congregations in that district, who should be able to master the set of skills required for that particular district in somewhere between ten and twenty years.

Setting a maximum term of office of six to eight years for a district superintendent may have been appropriate in 1955, but today that can be an influential component of any strategy designed to melt that ice cube. Another way to state the same point is, an arbitrary "one size fits all" limitation on the tenure of a district superintendent should be viewed simply as one more component of an obsolete and now dysfunctional system.

Another response to that "Why?" question is the 1968 merger clearly was a diversion from ministry, especially for the conferences from Pennsylvania to Missouri and Kansas. Another diversion consisted of the efforts in many annual conferences to reduce the unfunded liability in the pension system. Both of these became high priorities in conference planning.

Who Can Mobilize the Resources?

From this traveler's perspective, the most useful response to that "Why?" question is to shift to a larger perspective. All across American Protestantism the picture tends to be the same. The generations of adult churchgoers born after 1950 or 1960 can be found in disproportionately large numbers in the very large congregations averaging 700 to 800 or more at weekend worship. A majority of the congregations averaging fewer than 200 at worship are experiencing a decrease in their active constituency.

One part of the explanation is younger generations bring higher expectations and lower inherited institutional loyalties, as they shop for food, motor vehicles, homes, restaurants, schools for their children, clothes, communication equipment, entertainment, furniture, and bicycles. Add church to that list.

While many state they prefer a small congregation where everyone knows nearly everyone else, when decision-making time arrives, they often place a high value on quality, relevance, choices, and convenience. The dirty word for that is *consumerism*.

Others describe it as a "demand culture." Ailing patients demand same-day appointments with their primary care physician. Moviegoers demand that a new showing of that popular film begin every thirty minutes, not every two hours. Customers demand that the supermarket offer food ready to be heated and served. Banks have yielded to the demand of customers who want to be able to withdraw money at any hour of the day or night. The airlines have responded to the passengers' demand to be able to make a reservation and purchase a ticket at 3 A.M. More and more Christians who are members of first-day churches are demanding a weekend worship service be scheduled for the seventh day of the week. The Internet has responded to the demand by customers who want to shop from home in their pajamas at midnight. Colleges and universities have responded to the demand by students that only a few classes will be scheduled to begin before 9 A.M. Others have responded to the demand that a master's degree can be earned with only five or six weeks of time spent on that school's campus. The coffee bar in many churches today is designed to respond to the demand for an Internet connection with the worshiper's lap top computer.

The producer-driven American economy of 1955 has been replaced by the consumer-driven economy of today. One example is college and university dormitories, and the processes used for assigning roommates. One consequence for those planning for the future of their congregation is that the eighteen-year-olds of today may outlive today's fifty-five-year-old adults.

Many of those younger generations look for a church with a high quality set of ministries with children; an attractive youth program; a choice of four or five times, and three or four formats for the corporate worship of God; a variety of challenging learning opportunities for adults; several events and experiences that will enable them to meet and make friends with people like themselves; a surplus of accessible and safe offstreet parking places; challenging opportunities to be engaged in doing ministry; a future close friend from among the paid staff; air-conditioned meeting rooms; and inspiring sermons that nourish their spiritual pilgrimage.

While they may prefer a smaller congregation, many end up choosing a congregation that can mobilize the resources required to meet their expectations. One consequence is that a disproportionately large number choose a very large congregation. The new compromise is to offer them the intimacy of the midsized congregation along with the opportunities and experiences that only the large church can offer. This is the multisite congregation that averages 800 to 1,500 at weekend worship at the central campus, 350 at the west campus, 200 at the north campus, 450 at the south campus, 185 at the Jefferson Street campus, and 120 at the east campus.

Why should this long first chapter be devoted to a detailed description of the melting of that United Methodist ice cube? One reason is that the melting of the ice cube creates a fertile institutional environment for choosing up sides and drawing more lines in the sand—and that requires another chapter.

CHAPTER TWO

HOW MANY LINES IN THE SAND?

A major contribution of the book *United Methodism @ Risk* is that it draws a line in the sand. That line separates the "progressives," who advocate a more liberal approach to biblical interpretation, from the "conservatives," who defend the more traditional doctrinal statements found in the Articles of Religion in the Constitution of The United Methodist Church. *United Methodism @ Risk* also makes it clear that The United Methodist Church, like several other large Protestant denominations, also is in a battle over control. These are two reasons why it should be seen as an important book.

That is an accurate but incomplete interpretation of the current polarization within this denomination. From this observer's perspective that paragraph greatly oversimplifies what is really a far more complicated intradenominational quarrel. A more comprehensive diagnostic statement would begin with these five observations.

First, that highly divisive line in the sand over doctrine was drawn long before the first draft of the manuscript of the book @ *Risk* was completed.

Second, the teams (or interest groups or caucuses) on one side of one line may find several of their players are on the other side when the game is moved to a different playing field and another line in the sand is used to choose up sides.

Third, a reasonable guess is the vast majority of the laity and a majority of the parish pastors display little or no interest in choosing sides for a game of intradenominational quarreling. Many of those folks are far more interested in cooperating in a game called "Strengthening the Ministry and Outreach of Our Congregation." Another group prefer a game called "Taking Better Care of Our Current Members." (That raises the question of whether anyone will be left to read this book!)

Fourth, in the past three or four decades many different lines in The United Methodist Church sand have been drawn. One, for example, divided those EUB member congregations favoring a merger with the Methodist Church from those who refused to join the merged denomination. That line in the sand still exists. This traveler's observations suggest that tens of thousands of the members of the former EUB Church continue to be bitter about that merger. They still resent the dissolution and/or closing and/or sale and/or merger of hundreds of former EUB congregations, camps, schools, and other institutions. They regret the number of EUB ministers who left the parish ministry. Together they may account for close to one-half of 1 percent of the current membership of this denomination. On the other hand, perhaps as many as 5 percent of the current membership applaud the decision to merge. The remaining 95 percent tend to perceive that merger to be ancient and largely forgotten history.

That line in the sand is still there, and it is mentioned here only for one reason. It illustrates the fact that a combination of the passage of thirty-five years plus a couple of hundred thousand funerals can smooth over what once was a deep and divisive line in the sand. Will the passage of time and a million or so funerals smooth over the lines in the sand described in this chapter?

Fifth, and this is the excuse for writing this book, the publication and early response to @ *Risk* suggests the time has come to encourage open discussion of at least a score of other lines in the sand that already have been drawn. Rather than postpone these discussions for a decade or more, while that ice cube representing The United Methodist Church continues to shrink in the heat created by internal quarrels and external competition, it might be wiser to act while a substantial degree of institutional strength remains. The alternative of waiting and watching while tens of thousands of people reared in this religious tradition abandon what they perceive to be a sinking ship does not appeal to this observer.

This chapter invites the reader to take a side trip down a long road to get acquainted with several other lines in the United Methodist sand. This is not a requirement. Only an option. The purpose is to illustrate the point there is no easy solution that will win widespread support. If you already believe that, you may decide to skip this chapter.

Stay or Leave?

The line in the sand that has attracted the largest number of laity divides long-tenured United Methodists into two groups—those who have decided to stay, and those who have decided or are deciding to look for a different church home. Many of those who are leaving, and especially younger adults who are leaving behind parents, siblings, and friends, contend that for them this is the deepest and the most serious line in the sand; but there are many others. This line also illustrates the power of the right of self-determination, but more on that later.

This observer agrees that one of the most highly visible, the potentially most divisive, and the line that evokes the greatest emotion, is a central theme of @ *Risk*. Which approach to the interpretation of Holy Scripture should be the norm for United

Methodists? Will it be the "progressive" approach or the "conservative" position?

The Constitutional Crisis

A related deep and highly divisive line in the sand also is a central theme of @ *Risk*. Who will define that basic doctrinal stance for this denomination? A relatively small number of white males, all of whom have been dead for more than a century? Or, will every UM Christian be free to define his or her own belief system? Or, will that assignment be given to the Council of Bishops? Or the General Conference? Or a committee of seminary professors? Or a group of parish pastors? In broader terms, this line could be described as a quarrel over control.

That introduces what this observer is convinced is the deepest, widest, and most divisive line in the sand. That line can be described as a constitutional crisis. This quarrel is over both doctrine and polity. On one side of that line are those who contend, "This discussion was completed a long time ago. It no longer is open to debate. The constitution of The United Methodist Church is clear on our doctrinal position. In addition, our constitution is clear that our system of governance should be organized as a clergy-dominated and centralized command-and-control hierarchical structure. Those sections of the constitution cannot be amended! In addition, the leaders who negotiated the merger of 1939 did not choose the option of dissolving the three predecessor denominations and creating a completely new one with a fresh statement of doctrine and a new polity. That option also was rejected in the 1968 merger. That debate is closed. Every United Methodist has two choices: follow the way of the constitution, or take the highway marked 'Exit.' "

On the other side of that line in the sand are three groups. One declares, "Well, maybe the constitution can't be amended, but we can ignore it." A second group gently suggests, "We can live together if we redefine the issue. We all agree on the centrality of Scripture. The real debate is over the tools we use to interpret

Scripture such as tradition, experience, and reason."[1] The third group explains, "If the central purpose of our denomination is to quarrel with one another, we're leaving. Good-bye."

This internal quarrel over doctrine is far from new. One notable example came two centuries ago in the quarrel that led people to leave the Congregational Church and organize the Unitarian movement.[2] More recently, Episcopal Bishop John Shelby Spong challenged the central doctrinal statements of the Episcopal Church, USA and the Anglican Communion. Journalists have been taught that "when dog bites man, that is not news; but when man bites dog, that is news!" When a bishop preaches a sermon affirming the orthodox doctrinal position of that religious tradition, that is not news; but when a bishop goes on television to challenge the validity of the doctrinal positions of his church on the divinity of Jesus, the resurrection of Christ, and other central components of the faith, that is news![3]

What Is Ethically Acceptable?

The national publicity given Spong's views in the public media caused at least a few observers to draw a new line in the sand. Would it have been ethically acceptable in 1984 for someone to accept the full-time job as the director of campaign to elect Walter Mondale as the Democratic candidate for president of the United States, but in early October that person declare, "I do not believe in the platform on which Mondale is running, and I intend to vote to re-elect Ronald Reagan in November. However, I intend to continue in this position and to draw the paycheck I was promised when I took this job." While that never happened, would it have been ethically acceptable for that person to continue on the payroll of the Democratic campaign committee?

A similar issue arose in 2002 and 2003 when at least one editor of The New York Times declared the stories written by a young reporter were based on trips he never took and interviews he never conducted, but the Times continued to keep that reporter on the payroll and continued to publish his stories for many more months.

In 2002 and 2003 questions were raised about the ethical obligations of bishops in the Roman Catholic Church in America who were aware of the charges of pedophilia made against certain priests, but covered up those accusations, and those priests were continued on the payroll.

This line in the sand is the product of two questions. First, is it ethically acceptable for a person to accept generous compensation from an organization while publicly undermining the ideological and professional standards of that organization? Second, will continuing to keep that person on the payroll undermine the credibility of that organization?

On one side of this line in the sand are those who contend that freedom of speech, freedom of the press, freedom of the pulpit, and separation of church and state make this a moot issue. Next to them are those who argue that journalists and political figures should be held accountable to higher ethical standards than apply to the clergy. On the other side are those who are convinced that the ethical standards for the clergy should be at least as high as those by which journalists and political figures are evaluated.

Replaying the Protestant Reformation

For those who prefer not to describe this as a constitutional crisis, an equally divisive line in the sand is drawn over control. That also is a theme of @ *Risk*. One way to state it is "us" versus "them." This observer prefers to focus the discussion on the word *trust*. The Anglican Church was the creation of Henry VIII and his agent, Thomas Cromwell. The split with Rome was over control, not doctrine. Henry VIII clearly was an autocrat. On a spectrum of governance with the participatory democracy at one end, Henry VIII was within an inch or two of the other end. John Wesley was an autocrat who also believed in centralized control. It could be argued that distrust of local leadership, and the preference for a highly centralized command-and-control system is in the DNA of what today is The United Methodist Church.

It is only a slight exaggeration to suggest United Methodists are replaying the European Protestant Reformation five hundred years later in America. Can the laity be trusted? Or, is the church called to provide intermediaries between Christian believers and God? Is the Roman doctrine of papal infallibility replicated in the constitution of The United Methodist Church? Or, does each generation have the right to redefine both doctrine and polity?[4] Or, is it simply an issue of "our way or the highway"? This introduces a powerful force out of American history and the contemporary American culture.

The Cultural Line

The contemporary culture has fostered the growth of individualism[5] and a preference for voluntary partnerships over hierarchical structures. This is an expression of the larger dream of the right of self-determination. Europeans were motivated to immigrate to the new world to realize that dream of self-determination. During the past two centuries, tens of millions of immigrants have come to America to realize that dream. Young people left the farm to go to the city to be able to shape their own future. The capitalist economy is built on the foundation of self-determination. The American expression of a representative system of government is based on the right of self-determination.

One consequence is a deep line in the United Methodist sand is drawn on the basis of the application of this right of self-determination. One reason The United Methodist Church has been able to attract so few of the political liberals born after 1960 who place a high value on individualism is a polity that assumes an elite should rule the masses. That was acceptable in America until the arrival of Jacksonian democracy in 1828. Self-rule is a growing demand all across this nation today.

One big slice of the current debate can be summarized in three questions. Do congregations exist primarily to resource the denomination or to do ministry? Do the various denominational agencies exist to regulate local leadership or to resource congregations to enable them to expand their ministry? Should congregational leaders be trusted to make the policy decisions on such issues as the choice of their next pastor, human sexuality, the ultimate destination of their charitable dollars, the location of their meeting place, the system of governance for that congregation, the relationships with sister churches on other continents, the choice of music for use in the corporate worship of God, or in their staff configuration?

A negative response to this third question is appropriate if the top priority of this denomination is to reach, attract, and serve residents of the United States who were born before 1910. If, however, the decision is made to re-invent The United Methodist Church for ministry in the twenty-first century, the twin issues of governance and a better system of accountability to the constituencies must be a high priority.

If the future of American Methodism will be determined by those born after 1960 rather than those born before 1800, or even before 1950, it may be wise to count the survivors on either side of this line in the sand. One approach would be to count the number who favor a clergy-dominated central command-and-control system of governance for this denomination compared to those who believe the time has come to place greater trust in local leadership. Another would be to compare the number who have changed their religious affiliation at least once since age eighteen with those who are lifelong Methodists. (What do these have in common? Writing a book? Visiting a foreign country? Getting a divorce? Purchasing a motor vehicle? Committing murder? Changing careers? Switching churches? Answer: It's easier the second time!)

Perhaps the most useful indicator could be to determine the age of the living adults on either side of this line in the sand over trust, control, and the right of self-determination.

Covenant Community or Voluntary Association?

That debate brings us on this side trip to one of the most widely ignored, but also one of the most divisive issues, in the sands of American Protestantism. Is a Christian congregation a covenant community of believers who have gathered together around a clearly defined and fully shared belief system that is reinforced by a shared commitment to proclaim the gospel of Jesus Christ? Or, is it a voluntary association of individuals who share several common characteristics such as social class, skin color, language, place of birth or ancestry, inherited religious affiliation, and a desire to meet and make new friends?[6]

What's the difference? One basic difference is covenant communities usually have a relatively high and demanding threshold for admission, and a low and easy-to-cross threshold at the exit. (One exception is those covenant communities that require approval from superiors or from peers before a member may depart.)[7]

Voluntary associations usually have both a relatively low threshold for admission and a wide open back door for those deciding to leave. By definition, the members of a voluntary association retain the unilateral right of withdrawal.

This line in United Methodist sand attracts to one side those who believe this denomination should act like a covenant community, while on the other side are those who believe it is a voluntary association. On one side are those who contend, "Our system of ministers being appointed rather than called; our system of consumer-driven apportionments rather than donor-driven contributions; the reversionary clause in the title to the assets of congregations; the authority to ordain is in the denomination, not in congregations; the authority granted our bishops, and the whole concept of this being a connectional church are but a few of the many characteristics that are common to covenant communities. The only characteristic of our system that would suggest we are a voluntary association is lay members can withdraw without the approval of anyone."

The response from the other side is, "Those are not character-istics of a covenant community! Those are simply organizational patterns that have been adapted from the Roman Catholic Church. When a substantial majority of your members do not worship God with one of your congregations on the typical week-end, you can't call yourself a covenant community!"

Any plan to reinvent The United Methodist Church for the twenty-first century should include a decision on whether this will be a high-expectation/high-commitment covenant Christian community or a voluntary association of congregations. It will be difficult to play a new game if one group of players follow one rulebook, and other players on the team use a different rulebook.

Can You Politicize a Covenant Community?

Just down the road from that line of sand is a related one that has been bypassed by most of those looking for an interesting and challenging intradenominational quarrel. Here we encounter one of the most sophisticated arguments on this lengthy side trip. This line in the sand was drawn in several Protestant denomina-tions back in the 1960s. One of the reasons so many have bypassed it is the two sides tend to talk past each other. The line was drawn by those who advocated the politicization of the policy-making process in both the regional judicatories and national expressions of several American Protestant denominations. It is important to recall that the original context for the expansion of this quarrel was the 1960s. That was an era marked by protests against the war in Vietnam, the impact of the Civil Rights Movement, and several other liberating movements. College and university students were rebelling against their administrators.

One of the most influential pieces of legislation of the 1960s was the Economic Opportunity Act of 1964. Title II called for "the maximum feasible participation of residents of the areas and . . . groups served."[8] This legislation was supported by the propo-nents of participatory democracy and by those who saw a need to "empower the people."

A related expression of this same conviction was expressed by members of the Methodist Church. How can the people be empowered in a denomination that is organized as a clergy-dominated and highly centralized command-and-control system of governance? The obvious answer, contended those on one side of this line, is "Maximize the participation of the people. One way to accomplish that is to bypass the official power structure by organizing lobbies, interest groups, caucuses, and factions that can speak for those who are ignored by the power structures. The second way is to politicize the electoral processes that choose the delegates to General Conference, that elect the bishops, and that decide on the allocations of money in the denominational budgets. That's what is happening in cities all across the country. That's what's required by federal law in the administration of federal grants. That's what is happening in both the Democratic and Republican parties. That's also happening in the administration of the public schools. The time has come to empower the powerless, and that's why we need to politicize the decision-making processes in the Methodist Church!"

On the other side of that line were and are those who declare, "You've missed the crucial distinction between the Christian church and the federal government. The United States is a covenant community governed by the Constitution. While individuals and corporations retain the right to withdraw and take their assets with them, that right does not apply to the states. The states are the basic building block for this nation. That is reflected in the name—the United States of America. The parallel is, congregations are the basic building block for a denomination. You can have a theological seminary without a campus or students, but you can't have a denomination without congregations.

"Back in 1861–65 a great war was fought in this country over whether individual states retained the right of withdrawal. The war settled that question. The United States clearly is organized as a covenant community, not as a voluntary association. We do have thousands of interest groups, caucuses, and lobbies attempting to influence legislation, elections, and budgets, but we have a system of accountability built into the federal system of government. That also is true of most state governments. Authority and responsibility go together."

A notable exception that has received tremendous national publicity during the past twenty years is California. California is governed by the traditional three branches of government—executive, legislative, and judicial. The constitution, however, grants tremendous power directly to the people through the use of referenda and the recall. One consequence is chaos. One referendum placed a ceiling on general property taxes, but the people demanded more and better governmental services. One consequence has been described as "powerless hatred."[9]

Those objecting to the politicization of the annual conferences summarize their argument around three points. First, that would be completely acceptable if The United Methodist Church identified itself as a voluntary association of congregations and granted each congregation the unilateral right of withdrawal. Second, politicization could produce creative outcomes if the denomination and every annual conference were governed by the three branches of executive, legislative, and judicial, each with clearly defined authority and responsibilities, and a clear system of accountability that included at least quadrennial performance audits; but that is not the way the UMC is organized. Two of the big shortcomings in this denomination are the absence of an executive office or branch in both the annual conferences and the national structure, and the absence of the publicly reported annual performance audit. A third objection is, attempts to politicize the decision-making processes in a covenant community inevitably create that virus called "powerless hatred" among the losers.

Contribution or Mandate?

The next line has drawn a much larger crowd, and the emotional level of the debate is far more intense. On the surface, this quarrel is over apportionments. One side declares every congregation has an obligation to pay their apportionments in full. That is not negotiable! The other side asks, "Are you telling us apportionments are a higher priority than expanding the evangelistic ministry of our congregation?" Those on the pro apportionment side reply, "No! We believe you have the financial capability to do both."

A second facet of this argument is over the identification of the recipients of those apportionment dollars. The advocates of self-determination declare, "Those are our dollars that we contribute out of our tithes, and therefore we should be able to decide on the ultimate recipients of those dollars."

The defenders of the ecclesiastical economy of the 1920s and of apportionments explain, "Good stewardship demands that those apportionment dollars go to meet the greatest needs. The only way to determine that is if those who have a comprehensive view of all the needs and the criteria to define priorities make the decisions on the ultimate recipients. That's why we have a unified budget."

That evokes the response, "My translation of that is you don't trust the contributors."

Another critic complains, "I have a franchise for a fast-food restaurant. I pay a franchise tax every month, but in return I receive the counsel and many of the resources I need to operate my restaurant. My church pays our apportionments in full, but we don't get anything in return."

"That's the difference between Christianity and capitalism," comes the explanation. "As Christians, we are called to love others, to sacrifice on behalf of those in need, to share our blessings with others, and to return to the Lord the tithe that is his, not ours. Capitalists expect a return on every dollar of their investment, Christians give out of love, gratitude, and obedience."

A third perspective is offered by one who insists we take a long-term perspective in looking at apportionments: "This issue goes back a thousand years to when leaders in the Christian church in Europe concluded the saints in heaven had earned a surplus of merit. Part of that surplus could be transferred to living souls who had repented of their sins. By paying a sum to the church they could receive a remission of the temporal penalties for their sins. Pope Clement VI officially approved the payment of indulgences in 1343. Early in the sixteenth century a Dominican monk in Germany, Johann Tetzel, began to sell indulgences for the remission of sins of souls in purgatory. One-half of the money he collected was allocated to help pay for the reconstruction of St. Peter's Church in Rome. The only difference between indulgences and apportionments is indulgences were payments to win God's mercy, and apportionments are designed to win the favor of conference officials, the bishop, and the district superintendent. Both, however, have a long history behind them. This is not a new issue."

"But we're Protestants, not Catholics!" objected someone on the other side of the line. "Roman Catholic bishops still expect each parish to send to the diocese approximately 4 or 5 percent of that congregation's annual receipts, but our apportionments come closer to 8 or 9 percent."

Another participant in this emotional discussion raised another point. "You've missed one of the values in apportionments. They're needed for purposes of morale. In my conference we have a number of congregations that, year after year, report a decrease in church attendance, in baptisms, and in membership, so it helps when the pastor can announce in January, 'Last year, for the seventh consecutive year, we paid our apportionments in full.' Don't overlook the importance of morale. Every church needs at least one bragging point."

That debate never ends, but it really is about the differences between a voluntary association and a covenant community. It also illustrates the influence of the growth of individualism and the power of the right of self-determination.

Accountability? What's That?

The next stop on our side trip takes us to what was one of the most widely publicized lines in the UM sand in 2003. This quarrel erupted when the General Council on Finance and

Administration, which is charged with preparing a proposed expenditure budget for the World Service Fund and six other funds, asked national agencies receiving money from apportionments to describe the actual outcomes produced by the apportionment dollars they had received and spent. While this was not the language that was used, the request was for a performance audit. This is a widely used resource in the budgeting tool boxes of those responsible for budgets in state and local governments and in many nonprofit charitable agencies as well as in profit-driven corporations. It is an essential component of a system known as managing for results. It is *not* a new idea!

This result produced a new line in the UM sand. On one side are those who assumed this was and should be part of the normal budgeting process. They agree that if the decision is made to reinvent The United Methodist Church, governance and accountability must be high priorities.

On the other side were several agency heads and supporters who objected to this request. One objection was they were accountable to the General Council on Ministries, not to the General Council on Finance and Administration. A second objection was that never before had they been asked to provide a performance audit. A third was that it was too late to add this to the budgeting process. A fourth was the General Council on Finance and Administration was exceeding its authority in making this request for accountability.

When this former municipal budgeting officer read about this new line in the sand, my reaction was, "That's simply a natural, normal, and predictable outcome in a dysfunctional system that prefers to quarrel over inputs rather than be guided by outcomes."

Is the Ice Cube Really Melting?

While rarely discussed, one of the most significant of these lines in the United Methodist sand was introduced in the first chapter. Is our ice cube continuing to melt, or has it stabilized? On one side of this line are those who include the central conferences when they count and declare, "Our ice cube is not shrinking! Today it is larger than ever before!" On the other side are those who count only the UM congregations and congregations located within the United States and conclude, "Our ice cube continues to shrink."

Why Is It Shrinking?

If the focus is shifted from what the clergy enjoy quarreling over to comparing that shrinking UM ice cube with those now larger than ever before, three lines in the UM sand stand out in this explanation. The least widely discussed is in the answer to this question: What is the number-one point of commonality among the numerically growing congregations in American Protestantism today? From this observer's travels, the answer is not liberal or conservative. It is not mainline versus independent. The number-one point of commonality is, the numerically growing churches tend to project internally consistent and clearly defined high expectations of people. Some are at the liberal end of the theological spectrum. Others are in the fundamentalist camp. Most, however, are scattered along a broad middle section of that spectrum.

To be more specific, these congregations not only project high expectations of anyone seeking to become a member, they also offer specific challenges and equip the volunteers to accept that challenge. A common example of that high threshold into membership includes weekly participation in the corporate worship of God; weekly participation in a small group (personal growth or Bible study or prayer or connectional or spiritual growth or mutual support or ministry task force); at least one-half of that person's tithe returned to the Lord by way of that congregation's treasury; participation in a system designed to identify each individual's special gifts for ministry; and, eventually, participation in a ministry designed to equip one to utilize these gifts in ministry. This usually means offering worship experiences on both Sunday morning and at other times in order to accommodate those who have to work on Sunday morning to make a living. It also means customized responses for equipping and for participating in small groups. These high expectations are easier to project and fulfill in the self-identified covenant community than in a congregational culture resembling a voluntary association.

Typically these high-expectation congregations welcome anyone who wants to worship with them, but they maintain that high threshold into membership. One consequence is the average weekly worship attendance may be three or four or five or six times the membership.

Where is this line in the sand? On one side of this second line are those who are convinced it is relatively easy to become a high-expectation congregation in a denominational system organized as a low-expectation religious culture. The ratio of membership to average worship attendance in the UMC is approximately 5 to 2, not 1 to 3! On the other side of that line are those who believe it is possible, but extremely difficult, to create high-expectation congregations in a denomination that is organized with a low threshold into membership and a high threshold at the exit.

When the United Methodist institutional culture is contrasted with the culture of the larger and fast growing congregations in American Protestantism (including scores of very large UM congregations), a third line in the sand becomes visible. What are the key assumptions that drive the decision-making processes and determine the priorities in the allocation of scarce resources?

On one side of that line are those who are convinced that congregational leaders cannot be trusted. Therefore denominational leaders should define the denominational goals, operate the ministerial placement system, identify the ultimate destination of those dollars contributed by members to missional causes and, most important of all, require every congregation to be organized to help achieve the denominational goals.

On the other side of that line are those who operate on the assumption, "Our denominational systems exist not to expand employment opportunities for adults, but rather to encourage, support, and resource our congregations as they seek to fulfill the Great Commission. Our call is to resource, not to regulate!"

It is essential that both congregational and denominational leaders agree on the same guiding assumptions if the goal is to design a ministry plan for the twenty-first century.

Is the Appointment System Working?

A nearby line in the United Methodist sand relates to the size of that ice cube. What is one of the most influential points of commonality among the large congregations in American Protestantism? The answer is long pastorates. While long pastorates do not automatically produce large churches, it is rare to find a large Protestant church in America that has not benefited from a long pastorate. Is the UM system of ministerial placement working? On one side of that line is the sixty-year-old pastor who reflects, "This is my sixth appointment; and as I look back, I am very well satisfied with how the appointment system has taken care of me. The one time I felt I had to move, my new appointment was far better than the one I left."

A foot away stands the district superintendent or bishop who declares, "The biggest single threat to our system of itinerant preachers is the long pastorate!"

On the other side of this line in the sand is the volunteer leader who comments, "We joined this congregation thirty-two years ago. During these years we have had one exceptionally gifted pastor, but she left after only three years to go to a bigger church at a higher salary. Of the other six ministers who have served this church during our time here, one was good, but he was moved after only six years; two were okay; two were clearly below-average preachers, but one of the two was a widely appreciated loving shepherd; and the sixth was a disaster on all counts."

Standing next to that member is another layperson, who asks, "Should the top priority in the appointment process be to take care of ministers or to strengthen the health and vitality of congregations?"

To return to a point raised in the introduction, this is an especially crucial issue if one hope is to create a denominational culture that welcomes migrants from both Athens and Jerusalem. Could this denomination be reinvented to welcome and include both "progressives" and "conservatives" when the issue is the sources of authority for proclaiming the Christian faith? The history of schisms in Protestantism around the world during the twentieth century suggests one answer is, "Probably not."

Currently, when the train stops to replace the engineer reared in Jerusalem with one reared in Athens, a number of passengers conclude this is a good time for them to switch to another train. A few years later, when that train stops to replace that engineer with one from Jerusalem, another group of passengers also depart from that train. The more frequent those stops to switch engineers, the greater the number of vacant seats on that train.

A more optimistic response to the question above is, "Yes, if we recognize the importance of continuity within the culture of each congregation." When it comes to continuity in teaching and preaching, the number-one source, of course, is that parish pastor. Therefore if the goal is to reinvent this denomination as a theologically pluralistic religious body for the twenty-first century, one obvious requirement will be a strong affirmation of the right of self-determination. That almost certainly will include the replacement of geographically defined annual conferences with nongeographical affinity conferences. A second will be each congregation will be free to select its next pastor from a national inventory. A third will be the normative length for pastorates will be thirty to forty-five years.

That paragraph may motivate a few people to switch sides at this line in the sand.

Currently, on one side of that line are those who believe the normative length of a pastorate should be three to ten years, while on the other side are those who are convinced that fifteen years should be the minimum, and twenty or more years the norm, if one of the goals is to halt the melting of that ice cube.

Product or Service?

The next stop on our side trip finds a tiny crowd on either side of a line. On one side the signs read "Product." On the other side the people are carrying signs that read "Service." "What's this debate about?" we ask.

A person wearing a button with the word "Product" on it explains: "We believe our denomination is offering a product that should be uniform in content, high in quality, and the same wherever you go. That enables us to produce one set of resources that can be used by every congregation, one system of polity that fits every annual conference and congregation, and one organizational structure that can relate to every conference and congregation. If you're selling a product, uniformity is the name of the game. The McDonald's restaurant franchise made lots of millionaires by promising people uniformity of the product. That emphasis on uniformity and in the brand name explains how we have been able to continue our emphasis on short pastorates. Any elder should be able to manage any of the congregations in our chain of 35,000 franchises."

On the other side a United Methodist wearing a button with the word "Service" on it argues, "They're producer-driven. We're consumer-driven. We provide people with a service that we seek to customize in every one of our 35,000 congregations to match the needs, expectations, and priorities of people on a religious pilgrimage. Many of our churches, for example, do not offer the identical worship service three times on Sunday morning. They offer four or five different worship experiences every weekend, and each one is designed to meet the religious, personal, and family needs of one slice of the population. We have replaced the old concept of adult Sunday school classes with customized small learning communities, several of which do meet on Sunday morning, but two-thirds of them meet during the other one hundred sixty hours of the week.

"One consequence of being organized around producing a service rather than a uniform product is we have to place a high value on relationships. That is one reason our current senior minister in my church has been with us since long before the day we held our first public worship service twenty-eight years ago. That also explains why five of our seven full-time program staff are people who were lifted up out of our membership.

"Another consequence of our emphasis on service over product is we turn to outsiders rather than United Methodist vendors, as we purchase the resources we cannot develop by ourselves. The key sources of continuity here are not a denominational label on the building, or a parcel of real estate, or local traditions going back several decades, or kinship ties. The biggest elements of our continuity, as we serve a passing parade of people, most of whom were born after 1960, is in our mission statement, our role, our community image, our primary constituency, our small groups, our worldwide outreach, our equipping ministries, our community outreach, and our program staff, not in the geographical locations of our members' places of residence."

Defining Equitable

At our next stop we see a north-side line in the sand. The people on the east side are carrying signs with the word "Equity" on one side and a dollar sign on the reverse side. Those on the east side believe that the current generation of UM church members, unlike earlier generations, should accept the responsibility for fully funding the health insurance of the clergy who served their generations and are not retired.

On the west side of this line are those who are comfortable deferring to future generations of UM churchgoers the responsibility for a portion of those benefits earned back in the twentieth century. After all, that is the model for Social Security. This is simply one more intergenerational transfer of assets from younger Americans to benefit older generations.

The west side also is marked by signs with a dollar sign on one side and the word *equity* on the other. One definition of *equity* is to share the wealth. Therefore, instead of asking each congregation, or the pastor, to pay the full cost of that minister's health insurance, the conference pays the full cost for all ministers under appointment in that annual conference and recovers the current costs through apportionments. This could mean, for example, that the midsized congregation that is served by one full-time resident pastor and pays $20,000 annually in apportionments would have their minister's health insurance fully covered by apportionments. Five miles away is the meeting place of a large congregation with three full-time ministers on the staff. That church pays $140,000 a year in apportionments. The rich should help the poor.

On the east side of that line one person argues, "Health insurance should be seen as one component of a compensation package for a pastor that includes cash salary, housing, utilities, health insurance, that congregation's contribution to the minister's pension account, and continuing education. Therefore the full cost of health insurance should be paid by the people who currently benefit from that pastor's ministry."

A foot away is a layperson who has mastered elementary school arithmetic and is looking across that line in the sand to the people on the west side. "If you look at your policy as a reward system, it is obvious it calls for rewarding congregations for being relatively small and/or that have a below-average level of stewardship and/or do not pay their apportionments in full, while punishing larger churches and/or those with a higher level of stewardship and/or that pay their apportionments in full. Was that policy created as part of a larger strategy to encourage an increase in the number of small churches and to reduce the number of large congregations?"

"No!" shouts someone from the west side of that line, "The primary goal of this policy is equity!"

An economist on the east side explains, "Everyone knows that what we subsidize increases, but what we tax to pay those subsidies decreases."

Another person asks, "What is the unfunded liability for health insurance and pensions for the retired clergy?" No one on either side has an answer.

What Is the Wave of the Future?

At our next stop we are invited to share in a picnic lunch by several dozen United Methodists who have declared a one-hour truce in their debate. While we eat, they review some statistics for us that document the reason for this line in the sand. These data suggest that over the past three decades three of the outcomes of the present UM system have been (1) a reduction in the number of congregations reporting their average worship attendance from 37,641 in 1972 to 34,744 at the end of 2001, (2) an increase in the number reporting an average attendance of 19 or fewer from 3,839 in 1972 to 4,688 at the end of 2001, and (3) a decrease in the number averaging 100 or more at worship from 11,689 in 1972 to 9,925 at the end of 2001.

On one side of this line are those who contend, "Small is beautiful! People today prefer institutions organized to enhance interpersonal relationships, and the small church is a far better place to accomplish that than is the very large congregation filled with anonymity and complexity."

Among those on the other side of that line is one who says "I didn't know that!" and a second who declares "I don't believe it! In my annual conference we close an average of five small churches every year. How could that number be going up?" (Answer: That's easy. Larger congregations shrink in size to fit into this very small church bracket.) A third asks, "Where I live the number of Protestant megachurches has doubled during the past dozen years; so why have we not seen an increase in the number of large UM churches?" (Answer: We have in recent years. Back in 1965 at least 775 congregations in the two predecessor denominations reported an average worship attendance of 500 or more. That number plummeted to 432 in 1972, but by the end of 2001 it was up to an all-time high of 804.)

The UMC shrinkage has been in the middle—the percentage of all reporting congregations reporting an average worship attendance between 50 and 499 decreased from 56.6 percent in 1972 to 50.2 percent at the end of 2001. By contrast, the proportion averaging under 50 at worship increased from 40 percent to

45 percent, while the proportion averaging 500 or more at worship doubled from 1.1 percent in 1972 (down from 2 percent in 1965) to 2.3 percent in 2001. For comparison purposes it should be noted that between 4 and 5 percent of the rest of the congregations in American Protestantism average 500 or more at worship.

Whether those changes have been a response to carefully and precisely articulated goals by the several annual conferences or whether "that just happened" is impossible to determine. We do know that the number of American Protestant congregations averaging more than 500 at worship has more than doubled, and probably tripled, since 1960. As a group, the American-born Protestant churchgoers born after 1960 clearly prefer very large congregations, as do the migrants of all ages from the Roman Catholic Church in America.

As we prepare to resume our journey, we thank these gracious people for their hospitality, but one of our members asks for further clarification of this debate. "What's the central issue you folks are discussing?"

"Perhaps we failed to make it clear," came the courteous explanation. "Those on the other side are convinced the future niche for our denomination in American Protestantism is to increase the number of small United Methodist congregations. Our side contends we need to increase the number of midsized and large churches. The big argument, however, is over the definition of small. Does that mean congregations averaging fewer than 20 at worship, or those averaging fewer than 100?"[10]

Where Do We Go for Help?

For those who are concerned about the organizational structure of The United Methodist Church, the most divisive line in the sand may be in the response to this question: Where should congregational leaders go when they seek to learn how to do ministry effectively with new generations of American-born residents and with recent immigrants?

Currently, the answer includes parachurch organizations, denominational agencies, theological schools, books, videotapes, magazines, newsletters, conferences, workshops, church-related colleges and universities, the religion page of the weekly local newspaper, parish consultants, websites, teleconferences, printed case studies, retreat centers, academic journals, a couple of state universities, publishing houses, and entrepreneurial individuals.

From this observer's perspective the best answer is, "We're taking a team of leaders to a teaching church that several years ago resembled who and what we are today, but now is a model of the kind of congregation God is calling us to become in the years ahead." No alternative matches that in terms of relevance, credibility, authenticity, or pedagogy. The visitors listen to those who have done it, they ask questions, and they benefit from the second thoughts "but if we were doing that over again today, this is the way we would do it." The listeners meet a few leaders who are tall, handsome, intimidating, and unbelievably competent. Several members of the teaching staff that includes both professionals and lay volunteers, however, are short, fat, or ugly and have few quick and simple solutions to complicated problems. Most of the visitors go home convinced, "If they can do it, we can do it!"

What is the line in the sand? On one side are those who insist, "We need to allocate more money to enable our denominational staff to serve all types and sizes of congregations." On the other side are those who urge, "First, we need more of our most effective congregations to accept this role as a teaching church. Second, we need to create a website on which we list all the teaching churches we can identify that could resource our congregations. Our top priority as a denomination is not to create resources to meet all needs. We should broker the relevant resources that already exist!" (Does this idiot expect a denominational publishing house to publish his book?)

Who Are Our Peers?

The above paragraph introduces our tourists to one of the most interesting lines in the UM sand. It is interesting because tradition and rhetoric are well represented on one side, while contemporary activity dominates the other side. We begin by agreeing that one purpose of going to the traditional residence-based graduate school is, in the best of them, that is a place where graduate students learn from one another. Peers teach peers. Professors are hired to facilitate that process.

If you agree that a central purpose of denominational systems is to help congregations founded in the nineteenth and twentieth centuries design and implement a relevant ministry plan for the twenty-first century, one way to accomplish that is to create midlevel judicatories organized around affinity rather than the geographical location of the meeting places. For example, one conference could be designed to service circuits of three or more congregations served by one pastor. Another could be designed to serve circuits consisting of two congregations. A third could be designed to serve multisite congregations meeting at four or more locations, while another could serve congregations worshiping at two or three sites. One specialty conference could be for downtown churches averaging at least 350 at worship. Another could be for new missions launched during the two previous calendar years. At least two or three conferences could be designed for congregations meeting in Athens, and another two or three for those meeting in Jerusalem. Every year each congregation would be free to affiliate with the affinity conference the leaders believe would be most supportive of their ministry plan for the coming year.[11]

On one side of that line are those who believe a denominational official on a horse should not be expected to travel more than fifteen miles on the typical day. They are prepared to defend the traditional geographical boundaries of a regional judicatory. Your peers are your neighbors! That's what's wrong with teenagers. They identify with their peers rather than with the kids who live down the street.

On the other side are those who believe the privately owned motor vehicle will be commonplace for at least another two or three decades, and that travel by air is far cheaper, more widely available, and safer than it was in 1968 when many of the current conference boundaries were drawn. Most significant of all, an increasing proportion of UM congregations that create alliances to do ministry choose non-UM allies and/or they choose allies on the basis of affinity not geographical proximity. In addition, organizations such as the Leadership Network and the Willow Creek Association resource congregations and pastors without regard to denominational affiliation or geographical location. Websites on the Internet also provide resources without regard to denominational ties or location of the congregation's meeting place. Annual conferences and districts are among the last expression of the old concept that "People live where they sleep."

Do You Really Believe That?

The smallest crowd we meet on our tour is assembled on either side of a line in the Methodist sand that is rarely discussed. This line is based on the *Book of Discipline*, which charges the Council of Bishops with "the oversight of the spiritual and temporal affairs of the whole church." What does that mean?

On one side are a few people who believe the Council of Bishops should accept the role of responsible and initiating leaders in resolving the internal conflicts that have pushed such mandates as evangelism, missions, spreading Scriptural holiness across the land, and the spiritual and institutional health of congregations to a relatively low place on denominational agendas.

None of the nine people on the other side of this line share the same perspective. One declares, "That is asking the impossible of a group with severely limited authority." A second comments, "If the bishops cannot agree on a definition of the problem, how do you expect them to agree on a solution?" A third points out, "The *Book of Discipline* is the heart of our problem. It creates the illusion that we have a legislative branch in the General Conference, a judicial branch in the Judicial Council, and an executive branch in the Council of Bishops. How can you expect the Council of Bishops to lead when they can't even agree on the resurrection of Jesus Christ? The Council of Bishops should be abolished and replaced by an elected chief executive officer with the authority to lead, and a system to hold that individual accountable for what happens in this denomination."

A fourth says, "The problem is not the absence of leadership by the bishops; the problem is a dysfunctional organization." A fifth argues, "Everyone knows that in a big organization the civil service, not the elected leaders, decide what will happen. Why ask the impossible of the bishops?" Another suggests, "What we need is for the Council of Bishops to move the other leaders out of a state of denial into facing the fact that our denomination is confronted with a crisis. In three of our five jurisdictions we're retreating from the central cities and the older suburbs. The bishops should lead in planting new missions in urban America." A seventh asks, "Is anyone really expecting the Council of Bishops to lead in anything other than raising money?" The eighth of these nine observers contends, "The district superintendents, not the bishops, are the key to the future! They're the ones who develop district strategies and make the appointments required to implement that district strategy." The last member of this small group replies, "If you believe that, you're living in a different world than I inhabit. Let's go to lunch."

The discussion continues at lunch. Three agree that the bishops should lead this denomination in responding to the admonition in Matthew 25:34-45; three believe the Council of Bishops should make fulfilling the Great Commission in Matthew 28:19-20 the top priority; and three are convinced the time has come to discard that old wineskin and replace it with a new one customized for ministry in the twenty-first century.

One reason for the small crowd is several people who could contribute to this discussion are busy elsewhere writing articles or books on the role of the episcopacy, or working on proposals to expand the role of bishops.

One Site or Ten?

Several members of our party later agreed that the next stop turned out to produce the most challenging debate in our entire trip. To understand the existence of this line in the sand, we had to agree that 2010 is closer, in terms of time, than is 1995. The debate at this line is over the characteristics of a United Methodist congregation. Traditionally, these included a name that lifted up the denominational affiliation; a parcel of land with one or more buildings on it (in the North, a common pattern included the meetinghouse, one or two outdoor wooden privies, a shed for the horses, and perhaps a shed for storage of the wood required to heat the meetinghouse in the winter—but most of those outbuildings disappeared during the 1920s and 1930s); a congregation of at least a dozen adults (in 2001 only 1,663 UM congregations reported an average worship attendance of fewer than 12, up slightly from the 1,589 figure for 1986); a Sunday school; a minister who frequently was identified as "our preacher"; a unit of the United Methodist women; sermons delivered by a live preacher who was present in that room for that worship service; and a budget that included sending money to the conference treasurer. Many congregations also owned a parsonage, but today that is far from a universal pattern. The highly visible manifestation of the church was that parcel of real estate with a church building on it. A widely cited reference by local residents was, "The Methodist church is up on that hill" or "The Methodist church is located at the corner of Main Street and North Avenue."

During the past dozen years a small but rapidly growing number of American Protestant congregations have introduced a new model. (Actually, it is not a completely new model. A parallel model was developed by the Dutch Reformed Church in New York in the eighteenth century.) This model calls for one congregation meeting under one name, with one message, one identity, one governing board, one paid staff, one budget, and one treasury, with people gathering for the corporate worship of God at somewhere between two and two hundred fifty different locations every weekend.[12]

On one side of this line in the sand are those who declare, "We've never done it that way. Therefore the multisite option wouldn't work for us." Others point out the multisite option would allow one congregation to launch a new site that would intrude on the turf of an existing UM church. A common argument is that this would encourage members in these ten or fifteen sites owned by one congregation to direct their primary institutional loyalty toward that larger ministry rather than to the district or conference. A parallel criticism is that this would undermine the connectional system and the itinerancy. An elder on the staff of that large multisite ministry could be promoted several times without ever leaving that staff or asking the cabinet for a new appointment.

Those objecting to the multisite option have a strong case. This does threaten the status quo. It would undermine the dependency relationship thousands of small congregations currently have with their annual conference. It would transform the role and responsibilities of the district superintendent. It does require long pastorates. It probably would reverse that long-term operational strategy of increasing the number of small congregations. It would undermine the itinerancy. It would decrease the number of jobs for elders. It does expand local control. It does enhance the power of the laity. It does encourage congregations to build long-term and direct continuing relationships with sister churches on other continents rather than channeling those dollars and those short-term volunteer missionaries through the denominational system. It does mean a large proportion of the next generation of parish pastors will be prepared by working and studying in a multisite environment rather than on a seminary campus. It does mean only a minority of elders will be preparing and delivering sermons week after week. It does mean the power to launch new ministries at new locations will be exercised by congregational leaders rather than denominational officials. It could reduce the number of congregations closing each year to those few that chose dissolution over becoming the "west campus" or the "Jefferson Street campus" of a multisite ministry.

On the other side of that line are those who explain, "The success rate in adding a second or third site is far higher than the success rate in sending the dollars required to launch a new mission. In addition, it is easier to raise the money to expand our ministry than to raise money to pay apportionments." A couple of people add, "This model gives people the chance to have their cake and eat it. They can be a member of a small worshiping community organized around intimacy, caring, mutual support, and the absence of anonymity while being spiritually nourished by superb preaching and have full access to all the programs and opportunities to be equipped to do ministry that only the large church has the resources to offer." The treasurer points out, "The two big items in the budget of the typical small church are personnel and real estate. This model reduces those expenditures and allows us to allocate more money to ministry." Itinerant churchgoers rejoice, "This model enables me to change congregations without changing churches."

Do We Need Live Preachers?

This stop also produced a new line in the sand that polarized our guests. The discussions at that multisite congregation introduced what many will conclude is the most radical change taking place on the American church scene. Can you be there without going there? Hundreds of millions of people on this planet watched two commercial aircraft destroy two office buildings in New York City on September 11, 2001. For many that experience radically changed their perception of contemporary reality. More than 99 percent of those viewers were not even in New York State when that disaster took place, and the vast majority had never been in New York City.

My favorite example is a new Protestant congregation in Rockford, Illinois. They scheduled their first public worship service for July 18, 1998. One year later, Heartland Community Church celebrated their first anniversary with two firsts. For the first time in their history, two summer Sunday morning worship services brought a combined total of more than 1,600 worshipers. For the first time in their history the worship service included a live preacher. Before and ever since, the messages have been delivered by videotape. A second example is LIFE Church in

Edmond, Oklahoma. Founded in 1996, this congregation was averaging over 6,000 at worship in late 2003 with ten services at four sites. At six of those ten services, the sermon was delivered by videotape.

The demand for relevant preaching that combines a high level of competence in the messenger's communication skills with relevant content has never been greater in all of American church history. That demand far exceeds the supply.

In addition, the American economy has allocated tens of billions of dollars during the past half century training Americans how to receive important messages and to play games through moving visual images on a screen. One downside of that investment is that the proportion of American children ages six to fifteen who are obese has doubled during the past two decades. One upside is the low annual cost. This enables the self-identified missionary church to plant new worshiping communities at a variety of sites and to "adopt" small churches that are not able to attract and retain the services of a top-quality preacher. One messenger can deliver the good news of Jesus Christ in five hundred different worship services every weekend.

Implementation of this technology could enable The United Methodist Church to include 10,000 congregations in 2025 with weekend worship services in 75,000 places (that compares to 57,000 congregations in the six predecessor denominations in 1908) and a combined average worship attendance of 15 million (compared to 3.5 million in 2002). A reasonable projection would be one-half of those 10,000 UM congregations would be single-site congregations, each with its own full-time resident elder filling the roles of preacher, loving shepherd, administrator, teacher, counselor, fund raiser, evangelist, missions director, advocate for those in need, youth pastor, sacramentalist, prophetic voice, and community leader. The other 5,000 would be staffed by a combined total of perhaps 15,000 ordained elders, 10,000 laypersons preparing for ordination, several thousand diaconal ministers, and 85,000 part-time and full-time lay specialists. That scenario might require as many as five dozen district superintendents (ideally with a maximum tenure of twenty years in one district) and seven or eight bishops.

Which side of that line in the sand will you find yourself on five years from today?

Challenges or Strategies?

Finally, at our last stop on what several of our guests concluded should have been a two-day trip, we saw how contemporary administrative patterns have created two other lines in the Methodist sand. The first is, Do you favor challenges or strategies? One example is every four years the General Conference approves a goal for apportionments, but fails to design and approve the strategy required to achieve that goal. Each annual conference is assigned a goal and challenged to meet that goal. A second example is an annual conference or a bishop may challenge each congregation to increase its membership by 5 or 10 percent during the next year but not design and adopt the strategy required to achieve that goal.

Do you stand on the side of the line in the sand that believes numerical goals can and should stand alone? Do you believe that challenges issued by individuals and groups in positions of authority in hierarchical structures will be accepted and met by those located at a lower point in that hierarchical system? Do you believe these unilateral challenges will motivate others to design and implement their own strategy and the goal will be achieved?

Or, do you stand on the other side and agree that a goal without the appropriate strategy is largely empty rhetoric?

People or Systems?

A few feet away, the other line in the sand finds on one side those who are convinced the melting of that United Methodist ice cube can be blamed on incompetent pastors and/or irresponsible congregational leaders and/or denominational officials who really should be working full-time as greeters at the local Wal-mart. Those on this side agree that the need is to elect the "right people" to serve as delegates to General Conference, to be sure the "right people" are elected to the episcopacy, and to have "our people" dominate the policy-making operations in annual conferences and in the denominational agencies.

Or, do you stand on the other side of this very deep and exceptionally wide line in the sand with those who agree with W. Edwards Deming, that on this planet every system produces the results it is designed to produce? Instead of scapegoating people, and especially scapegoating parish pastors, a far more productive focus will be on (1) recognizing and accepting the fact that systems do produce the outcomes they are designed to produce, (2) achieving agreement on the desired outcomes, and (3) redesigning or replacing what has become a dysfunctional system with one designed to produce the desired outcomes.

Those on one side of this line are correct that it is easier, and also more fun, to scapegoat individuals than it is to restructure a dysfunctional system, but that is not the way to design the road that leads to a better tomorrow.

Five Popular Games

The last of these two dozen lines in the UM sand found four small clusters on one side, each playing a different game. Each of the four games had attracted several spectators. One group was playing a game called "Let's Identify the Real Scapegoats." The largest of these four groups was choosing up sides for a new round of a game called "Intradenominational Quarreling." A small group was playing a more complicated game called "What Are the Desirable Outcomes from Our System?" The smallest group was busy playing the game "Repairing Dysfunctional Systems."

On the other side of that line was a huge crowd of participants with only a handful of spectators passively watching. More than a million United Methodists were engaged in a game described simply as "Ministry, Missions, and Evangelism."

As we drove away, everyone on our tour agreed that last game was the most impressive experience of our entire tour. Several asked, "How can we enlist more people to play that game? It seems to us they were finding that to be a more fulfilling and rewarding experience than what was happening with the folk who were playing those four other games on the opposite side of that line."

As we continued our journey back to our starting place, it became apparent that most of our group were comfortable with two new skills: (1) building lists and (2) identifying lines in the United Methodist sand that we had failed to visit. Their composite list was the basis for complaints over what we had missed. After twenty minutes, that composite list included issues related to human sexuality; whether long-term financial subsidies nurture creativity or encourage dependency; the conflicts between Anglos and ethnic minorities over priorities; the role of women in the church; the responsibilities of district superintendents; whether the emergence of more megachurches should be encouraged or discouraged; the values and goals that drive American foreign policy; whether The United Methodist Church should declare itself to be one of the peace churches in American Christianity; whether the racial integration of congregations should be a high priority; whether youth ministries should focus on teenagers or on family constellations; how this denomination should lead in the alleviation of poverty; the role of the laity in ministry; racism; and whether new missions should be designed as large churches or utilize a model designed to produce congregations that probably will never exceed 135 in average worship attendance.

Our response was that we will discuss a few of those in subsequent chapters; so let's turn the page and check out the assumptions you bring to this discussion.

CHAPTER THREE

WHAT DO YOU BELIEVE?

I t is difficult to write the prescription for institutional renewal unless there is broad-based agreement on (1) the state of that institution's current health, (2) several assumptions about contemporary reality, and (3) at least a few of the tradeoffs that are a price tag on creating a new future. That introduces the first of a series of questions about a definition of contemporary reality and about the design of a strategy for the twenty-first century. Are most of the influential leaders in The United Methodist Church in agreement that this denomination is a healthy, strong, vital, mission-driven religious body; therefore no prescription is required? Or, is the required prescription treatment for an institution in denial? One reason for writing this book is the conviction that the best prescription for denial is to flood the system with information.

What is the most widely shared view among the more than one thousand delegates, denominational officials, and observers attending the 2004 General Conference? One expression of denial is, "Our denomination is a healthy and vital religious body, and there is no reason not to perpetuate the status quo!" Another form of denial is, "Our present system is the one we need to maintain; our problem is we need better people to staff it." A third diagnosis declares, "We do have a few problems, and the time has come to patch that old wineskin. Patches cost money, you know, so our top priority should be to raise more money to enable us to buy those patches." A more daring perspective concludes, "Let's face it, the time has come to replace that old wineskin with a new one."

If each of those four mutually exclusive options earns an affirmative response from one-fourth of the people at General Conference, you have wasted your time reading this far. If you are as optimistic about the potential future of this denomination as this observer is, you may want to reflect on a variety of questions about what you believe the future could or should bring. Several of these questions go back to the previous chapter to determine which side of those lines in the sand you find most comfortable. Most, however, focus on what you believe should influence the design of a strategy that will lead to a brighter future for this denomination.

Does Anyone Care?

Two important news items came out of the General Convention of the Episcopal Church USA in the summer of 2003. The most widely publicized was the controversy over the confirmation of the election of an openly gay and divorced priest to the office of bishop. For United Methodists, however, a far more relevant news item was the release of an extensive research report, *Restoring the Ties That Bind*.[1] One of the most positive notes in that report explains that Episcopal parishes are being revitalized by the arrival of adults who are on a self-identified spiritual journey. That is consistent with what this observer has gained from interviews with recent new adult members in scores of Presbyterian, United Methodist, Lutheran, Baptist, Episcopal, independent, and other congregations that are attracting substantial numbers of adult newcomers from outside their own religious tradition.

A second characteristic of these new adult members is they display little interest in what is or is not happening within that denominational system. The big exception to that generalization, which is emphasized in this Episcopal report, is the anger expressed when these members feel "local wisdom" is being ignored or when the denomination fails to encourage and resource local initiatives.

The most relevant finding was the discovery that a large number of the Episcopal laity display considerable indifference about what happens in denominational meetings. Their top priority is not the resolution of divisive intradenominational quarrels. Their top priority is nurturing the spiritual journeys of pilgrims on a religious quest.

This report raises a threatening question. What if the four options identified a few paragraphs earlier were increased to five, and the laity asked to choose their favorite? Would that fifth one win a majority of lay votes if it read, "Sell all of our old denominational wineskins, give the money to the poor, and do not purchase replacements"?

This writer is a strong denominationalist who believes the term "independent Christian church" is an oxymoron. I agree with Paul on the need for affirming the interdependence of Christian communities. Therefore we will stop chasing that rabbit after three paragraphs of caution.

First, this old man may be obsolete. It is possible the twenty-first–century response to Paul's emphasis on the interdependence of Christian congregations may not take the form of the traditional denomination. That call for cooperation and interdependence already is being answered by groups of congregations who identify themselves as alliances, associations, communions, conferences, conventions, fellowships, movements, networks, organizations, societies, synods, and unions. Many strongly deny they are denominations.

Second, it may be impossible to replace this old United Methodist wineskin with one new one. That long second chapter, which did overlook a few of the most divisive current lines in the United Methodist sand, was included to document a point. The combination of that large number of highly divisive intradenominational quarrels, plus the high level of emotion on both sides of several of the deepest and widest lines in the sand, plus the constitutional barriers may make it impossible to design one wineskin of sufficient size and strength to cover all these factions.

Third, pretend all of the United Methodists in the United States are gathered in one huge room with a dozen doors serving as exits from that room. One is marked "Exit here if you agree that the time has come to redesign the organizational structure of The United Methodist Church. Please *do not* use this exit if you are content with the present design or if you are convinced this is an irrelevant or potentially diversionary issue." Next to it is a door labeled "Exit here if you are ready to leave The United Methodist Church and search for a new church home outside this denomination."

We know that every year at least 200,000 United Methodists choose to pass through the second exit. At least one-half go to congregations that do not accept letters of transfer from congregations outside their religious tradition. One consequence is that thousands do not have their names removed from the membership roster of a UM congregation until long after they have departed. Many choose to worship elsewhere but do not become official members of what has become their new church home.

Which exit would attract the largest crowd?

How Much Uniformity?

How much uniformity should be built into a new system, regardless of whether the decision is to patch the old wineskin or replace it?

Do you believe one system of governance can be designed that will be appropriate for the 1,000 UM congregations averaging fewer than 10 at worship, and also work for the 800 averaging 500 or more at worship as well as the 1,000 averaging 36 to 39, and the 2,100 averaging 101 to 125 at worship? Or, should the new structure encourage each congregation to design a customized system of governance?

Next, do you expect every congregation should be able to implement a full-scale ministry plan? One outline for that annual audit of a congregation's performance in ministry consists of five categories. One purpose of that audit is to identify the actual allocation of all resources during the past year. That list of resources includes the time of paid staff, the time and energy of volunteer staff, money, the uses of the real estate, and, if appropriate, the use of denominational staff time and dollars. (For example, what proportion of the costs associated with the office of the district superintendent and/or conference staff were used to resource the ministries of this congregation? Please keep the tears generated by your laughter from falling on these pages!)

That outline includes these five categories:

1. Carrying out ministries for, with, and to our current constituency.
2. Transmitting the Christian faith to children and youth.
3. Helping to fulfill the Great Commission (Matthew 28:19-20).
4. Helping to provide social services and social justice ministries (Matthew 25:34-45).
5. Supporting denominational systems to hire others to do ministry on our behalf.

Do you assume one system for resourcing congregations, regardless of size and type, will enable all United Methodist congregations to be engaged in doing ministry in all of the first four of those five categories? Should every congregation be expected to allocate at least 10 percent of its resources to each one of those five categories? Or, should the system encourage one congregation to devote 85 percent of its resources to the first two areas of ministry while encouraging another to allocate 45 percent of its resources to fulfilling the Great Commission, and a third to concentrate 40 percent of its resources in responding to the call in Matthew 25:34-45?

Over there is a congregation worshiping in what today is a functionally obsolete building on an inadequate site at a poor location. Because of the cost of the capital improvements required to construct new facilities on a larger site at a better location, the leaders conclude they have two choices: "We can enlarge the size of the pie by a three-year building fund campaign that will be financed in part by contributions from accumulated wealth and allocate 43 percent of that larger pie to fulfilling the Great Commission, 55 percent to the first two categories, and divide the remaining 2 percent between the last two categories."

What do you believe the UM system should advise those leaders? Should the focus be on expanding the ministry of that congregation? Or, should the top priority be on funding the last two categories in that annual performance audit? Should the driving motivation be to increase the number of small congregations or to increase the number of larger churches? Should the system be designed to encourage congregations to hire others to do ministry on their behalf? Or, should congregations be encouraged to make expanding their own ministry the higher priority?

Here is a UM congregation currently paying $100,000 a year in apportionments. The leaders have been challenged to join nine other churches in that community to construct and operate a well-staffed shelter for homeless, single-parent mothers with young children. The annual subsidy for the first five years for capital expenditures and operating costs is estimated at $2 million. A local foundation has agreed to contribute $500,000 annually. The county has promised another $500,000. Each congregation will be expected to contribute $100,000 annually for five years as a response to Matthew 25:34-48.

The leaders of this congregation conclude they can raise $50,000 annually in designated second-mile giving for this venture. Should they reduce their payment on apportionments to $50,000 a year and join the coalition? Or, should they reply "Sorry, but we can't afford it"?

Can We Compete in a Free Market?

Those two examples introduce what many readers will conclude is the most divisive issue to be raised in this chapter.

The context for this discussion requires another brief side trip. This one takes us back nearly eighty-five years in the history of contemporary American Methodism. One of the greatest chapters in the history of American Methodism was initiated during World War I.[2] Leaders in the northern church invited the southern church to join in a celebration of one hundred years of missionary work. That led to the launching of the Centenary Campaign of 1919. The goal was to raise millions of dollars for foreign missions, for home missions, and for relief work in a Europe devastated by war. More than a million Methodists from all over the nation traveled to Columbus, Ohio, in the summer of 1919 to launch this missions-driven campaign. The request for volunteers to staff the campaign motivated 100,000 "minutemen" to enlist. Pledges totaling nearly $150 million were secured. The amount actually received, however, came to approximately $105 million.

How much was $105 million in 1922? The Consumer Price Index for 2003 stood at 184 compared to 16.3 in 1922. That means $105 million in 1922 had the purchasing power of $1.2 billion in 2003. In 1922 one-third of 1 percent of the budgeted expenditures for the federal government was $110 million. In 2003 one-third of 1 percent of the federal budget was $7 billion.

Could The United Methodist Church raise even $1 billion in 2004 for missions and world relief? Yes! That goal could be achieved if the pleas for money for these attractive causes were delivered as persuasive messages by trusted messengers in a denomination not polarized by internal quarreling.

Was the Centenary Campaign a success or failure? One consequence was the word *centenary* became a popular first name for new missions organized in that era. Many of the leaders of that era were disappointed. At least a few described the Centenary Campaign as a failure.

This observer defines it as a success story. One reason all the pledges were not fulfilled was the economic depression in agriculture that began in 1922. A large proportion of Methodists in 1922 were members of rural and small-town congregations where farming was the core of the local economic base. A second reason was the national euphoria of 1919, when that large rally was held in Columbus, Ohio, had begun to dissipate by 1920.

A third factor was that both denominations already were well along in the process of switching from expansion to retrenchment. The series of censuses of religious bodies conducted by the United States Bureau of the Census in 1906, 1916, 1926, and 1936 reported a total of 29,943 congregations in the northern church and 17,831 in the southern church in 1906. In 1916 those numbers were about the same—29,342 and 19,220. By 1926, however, both had dropped to 26,130 and 18,096, respectively. During the next decade those numbers plunged to 18,340 congregations in the northern church, and 11,454 in the southern. (The Methodist Protestant Church also cut back from 2,825 congregations in 1906 to 2,473 in 1916, to 2,239 in 1926, to 1,498 in 1936.)

Concurrently, the Church of the United Brethren in Christ cut back from 3,699 congregations in 1906 to 3,481 in 1916, to 2,988 in 1926, to 2,500 in 1936. The Evangelical Church—the result of the reunion of two denominations—reported a combined total of 2,738 congregations in 1906 and 2,570 in 1916. The reunited denomination included 2,054 congregations in 1926 and 1,895 in 1936.

As The United Methodist Church has demonstrated in recent decades, raising money for national denominational agencies to spend while concurrently reducing the number of congregations may not be mutually reinforcing goals.

A fourth part of the explanation for many of those pledges to the Centenary Campaign not being fulfilled was Methodist congregations also were the recipients of direct appeals from a variety of national and conference agencies asking for money. That playing field was overflowing with aggressive players. While other factors also were at work, one consequence was the creation of the World Service Commission in 1924. The goal was a unified budget to fund the ministries of all the national agencies. Efficiency, economy of effort, and equity were among the goals. The old system opened the door to the most persuasive messengers raising the most money. The new system was designed to give a high priority to the most meritorious causes. The old system allowed the donors to direct where their contributions would go. The new system enabled those officials with an informed and comprehensive view of all the needs to define a fair and equitable distribution of limited financial resources.

Most of the next two decades in American history were years of scarcity rather than abundance, and that rationing system fit the American economy. The door was reopened for designated giving in 1944 when the Crusade for Christ was adopted. Four years later that door for designated second-mile giving was opened permanently with the adoption of Advance for Christ and His Church. The competition for the charitable dollar was legitimatized.

While rarely stated this bluntly, it was widely assumed that the national agencies of the Methodist Church could not and should not plan to fund their budgets by fees for the goods and services they provided to congregations and conferences. A financial subsidy was required. The big exception to that generalization was the United Methodist Publishing House.

Concurrently, that playing field was expanding, as a variety of parachurch organizations and other nondenominational agencies and causes entered the game. By the 1970s a rapidly growing number of entrepreneurial individuals, retreat centers, parachurch organizations, independent publishing houses, for-profit corporations, teaching churches, state universities, theological schools, parish consultants, research centers, and fund-raisers were beginning to compete in that ecclesiastical marketplace. Most were organized to provide goods and services for congregations. Several also identified denominational systems as part of their market, especially the regional judicatories that did not feel they were being resourced adequately by their denominational system. Many of these new competitors depended on financial subsidies from individuals, congregations, governmental agencies, denominations, or foundations to balance their budget. Others, however, were able to pay all their bills out of receipts from the sales of their goods and services.

That raises a crucial question in designing the future. Do you believe the national denominational agencies can and should be financed by user fees? Or, do you believe they can and should depend on both user fees plus funds they solicit from foundations, governmental agencies, individuals, and congregations? Or, do you assume most will need a continuing financial subsidy from what we currently call "apportionments"?

Distrust or Self-determination?

What is the difference between the Roman Catholic Church in America and the United Church of Christ?

One huge difference can be found in Article V of the constitution of the United Church of Christ (UCC). The UCC closely resembles a voluntary association of autonomous congregations, associations, conferences, boards, and other national denominational agencies. Paragraph 9 of the UCC constitution declares, "The basic unit of the life and organization of the United Church of Christ is the Local Church." That is followed by a four-line Trinitarian doctrinal statement. Paragraph 18 begins with the declaration, "The autonomy of the Local Church is inherent and modifiable only by its own action." That paragraph goes on to define in detail that congregations have the unreserved authority to make their own decisions on everything from their confession of faith to control over all assets to the unilateral right to withdraw from the denomination.

The polity of the Roman Catholic Church is based on distrust of local leadership. The polity of the UCC is based on unqualified trust of local leaders. The Roman Catholic Church resembles a high-commitment covenant community in which the members surrender most of the right of self-determination. It also is organized around the principle the people and the parish priests *cannot* be trusted on matters of either doctrine or polity. The United Church of Christ is organized on the assumption the people can be trusted on issues of both doctrine and polity.

The Restrictive Rules in the constitution of The United Methodist Church were based on the assumption in the early 1800s that future generations could not be trusted on the core issues of either doctrine or polity.

What do you believe should drive the planning for the future of this denomination? You have five choices.

1. I believe current generations cannot be trusted on the core issues of both doctrine and polity.
2. I believe the only people we can trust on doctrine are those who are dead, but we can trust present and future generations to design a polity that is appropriate for the twenty-first century.
3. I believe we can trust the present generations to write a new doctrinal statement for our denomination, but we must continue our historic episcopal polity.
4. I believe we can trust present and future generations to make whatever changes they conclude are appropriate on both doctrine and polity as the need arises periodically to reinvent this denomination.
5. I believe this book was published to prove the devil is alive and at work in our denomination, and that is the reason I am leaving to join a congregation in another religious tradition where the top of the agenda is not quarreling but is ministry, evangelism, and missions.

The last two options on that list represent a vote for self-determination. The first three represent choices based on varying degrees of distrust. Which should guide the planning for the future of this denomination? If you are completely addicted to intradenominational quarreling, choose one of the first three.

How Much Self-determination?

If you assume that any future organizational structure will permit individuals, pastors, congregations, denominational officials, annual conferences, and denominational agencies to exercise a greater degree of self-determination, do you favor creating some boundaries?

The front-page example in mid-2003 was whether the members of a diocese in the Episcopal Church USA were free to choose their own bishop. Or must that election be confirmed by one other body in the denomination? Or by both of two other bodies?

That represents a central thread in several facets of American life. Does a patient have a right for a second opinion from another medical expert on his or her illness? Can the ruling of a judge or jury be appealed? Do both houses of the United States have to approve proposed legislation before it is sent to the president for approval or a veto? Can a sixteen-year-old appeal the decision of one parent to the other parent?

The general theme of the American culture is based on the assumption that human beings do err. It assumes the doctrine of original sin continues to be valid. It assumes the right of self-determination also includes the right of others to appeal their decision. That explains the existence of the Judicial Council in The United Methodist Church.

Two questions remain without universally agreed-upon answers: (1) Can the decisions of generations long since dead be appealed? (2) What happens if a person joins a religious community, vows to uphold both the doctrine and the polity of that religious community, and also understands that neither the core components of the doctrine nor the polity can be changed, but subsequently disagrees with the doctrine and/or the polity? If no provision for an appeal exists, what are the options? To ignore those earlier vows? To leave quietly? To claim "I didn't know what I was agreeing to when I took that vow, and therefore I don't have to uphold what I don't believe"? To publicly protest the validity of the doctrine? To build support for changing the polity? To pretend "We don't have a problem"? Or to declare that individuals have the right of self-determination, while institutions are limited by self-imposed rules on the right of self-determination?

If you conclude that The United Methodist Church is a covenant community organized around high expectations, you will come to a different conclusion than if you believe it is a voluntary association of more or less like-minded people with a few shared goals.

Covenant Community or Voluntary Association?

That brief paragraph introduces what this observer is convinced is one of the crucial lines in the UM sand, but also one of the most widely ignored. Should the organizational design for the future be based on the assumption this denomination is and should continue to be a covenant community? Or, should it be based on the assumption this denomination closely resembles a voluntary association of people with a shared heritage?

One example of a voluntary association was and is the societies created by and for the benefit of immigrants to the United States. A second are the veterans' organizations such as the one for the Yankee veterans of the Civil War. A third is the service club. A fourth is the 4-H Club. A fifth is a political party. One common characteristic is the unilateral right of withdrawal. The Southern Baptist Convention, the Evangelical Lutheran Church in America, and the United Church of Christ all resemble voluntary associations of congregations.[3]

Contemporary examples of high-commitment covenant communities include the Special Forces in the United States military, hundreds of high-expectation and high-commitment nondenominational American Protestant congregations, the Church of Jesus Christ of Latter-day Saints, the United States Marine Corps,[4] and the Society of Jesus.

From this observer's perspective it appears the Methodist Church of 1815 was organized as a high-expectation, high-commitment Christian covenant community. During the next fifteen to sixteen decades, however, it accelerated the process of evolving into a voluntary association that has become, as voluntary associations often do, an increasingly legalistic institution.

What do you believe it is today? What do you believe it should become in the years ahead?

What Changed the Agenda?

If one measures outcomes for a period of at least fifteen years in the late 1940s through the early 1960s, the system of the former Methodist Church clearly was designed to reach more people with the gospel of Jesus Christ. Between 1951 and 1965 the combined confirmed and preparatory membership in the United States increased from slightly over 10 million to nearly 12.2 million. An average of more than a hundred new congregations were organized each year. The work in other parts of the world was expanding. In the United States, Sunday school attendance increased by 20 percent in fifteen years. Each year more than 300,000 new members were received annually by profession of faith. Baptisms ran between 300,000 and 400,000 each year. Two new seminaries were opened. The number of episcopal areas was increased. Additional conference and national staff were hired. The Woman's Society of Christian Service reported approximately 1.7 million to 1.8 million members year after year—twice the number in recent years.

What happened? What do you believe produced a change in the outcomes produced by the Methodist system? What do you believe has moved intradenominational quarreling to such a high priority on the current agenda? One cause, of course, as is

104

described in a previous chapter has been death. Most of the members and policymakers of 1950 have died.

Another part of the explanation, as is pointed out repeatedly in this book, is that other concerns have pushed new church development and evangelism to a lower place on denominational agendas. Another was the aging of congregations. Congregations that have been meeting at the same address for more than forty years are far less likely to attract younger generations than are new churches.

Another set of factors surface if that "Why?" question is narrowed down to "Why have so many lines been drawn in the United Methodist sand in recent years?" High on the list is the rise of individualism:[5] "I have a right to my own opinion on that subject." The culture of the United States during the past half century has affirmed that right. One price tag has been the erosion of the authority that went with the office for police officers, professors, pastors, physicians, presidents, bishops, and other bosses. The rise of individualism has undermined the sense of connectionalism in this denomination. The rise of individualism also has fed the fires of internal conflict in a variety of institutions, including universities,[6] community organizations, the United States Congress, and The United Methodist Church.

Another slice of the explanation lies in that evolution from a covenant community into a voluntary association. That change has coincided with a parallel shift in the American culture. Vertical organizational structures are being replaced by horizontal partnerships. A vertical change of command is an asset in fighting a traditional war, but that structure in a voluntary organization creates a fertile environment for internal conflict.

A rarely discussed factor is, for at least three or four decades the theological pendulum in the United States was swinging from conservative to liberal. During the past two or three decades, younger generations have been pushing that pendulum in American Protestantism in a more conservative direction. In the Roman Catholic Church, that pendulum clearly moved in a more liberal direction from the 1950s through the 1970s; but the past two decades have seen it swing back in a more conservative direction. Whenever that pendulum reverses its direction, one predictable consequence is an increase in intradenominational quarreling.

Another pendulum reversed direction three times during the twentieth century. From 1917 through 1929 the national pendulum swung in the direction of greater unity. From 1929 to 1941 it reversed and swung in the direction of partisanship and bitter public criticisms of those in positions of authority and on the direction of both American domestic policy and American foreign policy. A reversal came in December 1941, and for at least fifteen to eighteen years this national pendulum reversed direction and swung in the direction of national unity. It is not a coincidence that also was an era when the Methodist Church reached a peak in numbers.

The 1960s saw that national pendulum begin to reverse direction. Partisanship, conflict over national goals and public policies, investigative journalism, and demands for participatory democracy encouraged public quarrels. That also was the era when the decision was made to politicize the decision-making processes in several annual conferences. Those were among the forces that encouraged Americans to choose sides on a huge number of issues. In recent years that has been facilitated by the Internet, which provides a low-cost channel for fanning the flames of dissent.

Finally, and many readers will place this at the top of this list of factors, is a significant difference between winners and losers. One high school basketball team won its fourteenth consecutive game one night. They defeated a team that lost for the twelfth time in its fourteen games. Which team enjoys a high level of unity and cohesiveness? Which coach is criticized for "not being able to relate to today's teenagers"?

A large corporation with 1,200 retail stores reported that for the fourth consecutive year every store reported an increase in profits. In another corporation, for the third consecutive year a majority of retail outlets reported their profits had dropped from the previous year. Which corporation displays the greatest tolerance for mavericks? Which corporation is now engaged in a search for scapegoats? Which corporation hires consultants to come in and help identify and solve their problems?

The basic generalization is that numerically growing institutions are better able to tolerate, and even benefit from, internal dissent than are numerically shrinking institutions. The numerically growing institution provides a favorable environment for reinforcing a feeling of unity, while the numerically shrinking institution provides an environment that encourages the search for scapegoats, for finger pointing, for choosing sides, for internal quarrels, and for drawing more lines in the sand.

What do you believe have been the most influential forces behind the recent rise in the level and intensity of intradenominational quarreling? Your response to that diagnostic question will help you write the appropriate prescription.

What Do You Call It?

The name we place on anything influences our conceptual framework for subsequent discussions. One single family residence may be called a cottage, while another one a mile away may be identified as a mansion. Should those spots on the skin be called chicken pox or smallpox?

Currently, a variety of words are being used to describe the relationship of congregational leaders to their denominational system. A highly influential leader in the Evangelical Lutheran Church in America has described it as disengagement. A Southern Baptist labels it localism. One Roman Catholic priest uses the word *alienation*. (In the last essay in chapter 4, Norman Neaves discusses this issue.)

In this book, and on other occasions, my preference for positive terminology has motivated me to use the word *self-determination*. That, however, can create confusion. A useful distinction is between causes and consequences. Words such as *disconnect* or *disengagement* or *alienation* describe a condition. Self-determination can be described as a goal or a movement. In a colonial system the drive by the people to attain the right of self-determination naturally tends to create a condition known as adversarial relationships. An internal quarrel over control usually is expressed in the growth of adversarial relationships that may be described as hostility.

In one discussion on this subject a laywoman commented, "My definition of the condition is apathy. I believe that is a natural consequence of projecting low expectations. I coach a girls' soccer team, and we expect to win every game. That creates an unhealthy environment for apathy. In my annual conference, apportionments are used to reward mediocrity and to punish success."

Likewise, undesirable outcomes are a natural and predictable outcome of a dysfunctional system. Undesirable outcomes often produce a hostile relationship between those providing the resources for that system and those operating the system. In California that has been described as "taxpayer revolt." In The United Methodist Church, that may produce a condition described as "disloyalty," when a large congregation refuses to pay its apportionments in full and diverts those dollars to other missional endeavors.

The issue of terminology is less important than a half dozen questions evoked by this discussion.

First, do you believe words such as *disengagement, apathy, disloyalty,* and *localism* refer to a serious internal problem? Or, do you agree they really describe consequences or symptoms, and the focus should be on the causes rather than the consequences?

Second, if these words do describe consequences, what do you believe are the root causes that produce these consequences?

Third, do you identify that cause as a serious problem? Or, does it rank about ninth on your list of the dozen most urgent issues confronting this denomination?

Fourth, is that system identified as your annual conference designed to evoke loyalty, enthusiastic support, and cooperation from congregational leaders? Or, is it designed to produce apathy, disengagement, and hostility?

Fifth, if you have concluded disengagement and apathy have increased to the point of becoming a serious problem, what do you believe should be the remedy for this condition?

Finally, if you are becoming increasingly bored with this whole discussion, are you about to declare, "The correct word is *indifference!* That's why I've decided to stop reading this book!" (Incidentally, that is a completely acceptable response, if you purchased this copy. If you borrowed it, you should return it to the owner.)

Geography or Affinity?

The United Methodist organizational structure for the United States divides the system into five layers. The largest layer consists of the entire denomination—congregations, districts, conferences, jurisdictions, and a number of denominational agencies. The least noticed are the five geographically defined jurisdictions. These consist of the geographically defined annual conferences, plus two missionary conferences (Alaska and Red Bird), plus two ethnic conferences. Congregations and missions not yet constituted as organized churches constitute the fifth layer.

The beginning question in defining the future is, What is expected of the annual conferences? Are they expected to regulate congregations and pastors? To redistribute wealth and income? To elect delegates to the General Conference? To resource congregations? To serve as the cornerstone for ecumenical relationships? To raise money to help finance ministries on other continents through a direct relationship that bypasses the General Board of Global Ministries? To serve as a prophetic voice for the congregations and members in that annual conference? To create, fund, and operate social service agencies? To enlist people for full-time Christian vocations? To relieve congregations of the burden of finding a replacement for their current pastor? To fund and administer a variety of benefits for the clergy? To close redundant and unneeded or failing congregations? To plan and administer meetings? To plant new missions? To recruit ordained ministers from elsewhere to serve in that annual conference? To counsel pastors? To help congregations design and implement a customized ministry plan? To enable congregational leaders to learn from the leaders in similar congregations? The annual performance audit will reveal the percentages of resources devoted to each of these and to other roles.

Which should be the top priority in the allocation of scarce resources? Which organizational structure will be most useful in implementing the top priority? This observer is convinced that enabling congregational leaders to learn from one another how to "do church in the twenty-first century" should be a very high priority, and the affinity conference is the best way to do that.[7]

What do you believe? If an effort is made to reinvent this branch of American Methodism, should the conferences be defined by geographical boundaries, or as associations of similar congregations?

Inclusive or Exclusionary?

This issue requires drawing a line between the Christian faith as a world religion and that institutional expression of the Christian faith we Americans call congregations and denominations.

Repeatedly Jesus made clear statements that declare a high threshold exists for those who want to become Christ followers. By definition, Christianity is a high-expectation religion. The door to become a follower is wide open, but the entrance threshold is high. The rear threshold for backsliders to leave is low. The parable of the rich young ruler and the warning not to try to be loyal to two masters are but two of many examples. Christianity is an exclusionary religion.

Thousands of gatherings of Christians have focused on the question "Whom should we exclude?" One of the first is described in Acts 15:1-11. One of the more recent of these gatherings was the triennial convention of the Episcopal Church USA, held in the summer of 2003. Bishops in the Roman Catholic Church in America have been meeting in recent years about the proposed exclusion of priests who are pedophiles. Another example is the question of whether divorced and remarried Christians should be excluded from the sacrament of Holy Communion. Several religious bodies exclude anyone who volunteers to serve in military combat. Others exclude adults who use tobacco or alcoholic beverages.

Currently, one of the most divisive debates in America is over the frequently heard comment, "Christians, Jews, and Muslims should be able to get along. All three religions worship the same God." Jesus said, "I am the way, and the truth, and the life. No one comes to the Father except through me" (John 14:6).

For Christians and Jews, that hope for a friendly relationship was reinforced by a statement from the Roman Catholic Church at the Second Vatican Council. It described the two covenants with God, one in what we call the Old Testament and the second in the New Testament. The Koran, however, is categorical. There is only one God and one covenant. Do you believe Christians and Jews can come together to worship God? Do you believe Jews, Christians, and Muslims can gather together in the corporate worship of one God? Or, do you believe the exclusive character of each of those religions makes that impossible? This debate is almost certain to heat up in early 2004 with the release of Mel Gibson's powerful motion picture on the death of Christ.

This discussion introduces a critical issue for those responsible for reinventing The United Methodist Church for the twenty-first century. Should The United Methodist Church be designed on the assumption that every congregation can, should, and will be an inclusive fellowship that welcomes everyone who (1) accepts Jesus Christ as Lord and Savior or (2) is on a self-identified religious pilgrimage and is open to that possibility? Should every UM congregation be prepared to welcome and serve everyone, including those who believe in the Old Testament God as the Creator but reject the divinity of Jesus and reject the belief that Christ died on the cross, on the third day was resurrected from the dead, and now is with God the Father? Should every UM congregation be expected to welcome, accept into full membership, and continue in full membership those believers who participate in the corporate worship of God in that particular Christian community at least once or twice a year but never as frequently as five or ten times a year? Does golf, shopping, travel, soccer, and fishing rank above worship on the list of priorities of United Methodists?

In summary, do you believe The United Methodist Church in the twenty-first century should place a high priority on inclusiveness and a low priority on commitment? The answer "We can do both" will require a drastic revision of the rituals followed in baptisms, the reception of new members, the celebration of the sacrament of Holy Communion, and the ordination of future ministers. Replacing the acceptable responses in the current rituals with "It all depends" probably will be a vote to continue the melting of that ice cube.

Church or Association?

One Tuesday morning the telephone rang in a building housing a Southern Baptist congregation. The church secretary was away from her desk, so the pastor answered the phone. "Good morning! This is the Davis Street Baptist Church. How can I help you?"

The voice on the other end of the phone line responded, "Oops! I'm sorry. I must have the wrong number. I was calling the Southern Baptist headquarters."

The pastor replied, emphasizing the word *is*. "This *is* the Southern Baptist headquarters. How can I help you?"

This conversation, which is now a legend in the oral tradition of the Southern Baptist Convention, introduces a pivotal question. If and when The United Methodist Church is reinvented, should it be defined as a "church" in the same definition of that word as is used in the Anglican Communion and in the Roman Catholic Church? In both of these religious traditions, the doctrine and the polity are both defined by headquarters, often by long-dead white males. Questions about either doctrine or polity are resolved back at headquarters.

The United Methodist heritage traces back to the Roman Catholic Church and the Anglican Communion, not to American

Protestantism. After all, John Wesley was an Anglican priest and a lifelong loyal member of the Church of England, not a Protestant minister. Should this denomination be reinvented as a voluntary association of American Protestant congregations? Or as a church consisting of a federation of annual conferences? Which do you believe would be the most promising road to the renewal of what has become a failing system for both the Roman Catholic Church in America and The United Methodist Church in America?

This tension between a denomination describing itself as a church rather than as an association, conference, or convention of congregations and other organizations can be seen most clearly in the contemporary intrachurch quarrel within the Southern Baptist Convention (SBC). As recently as 1975 the SBC was organized as a convention of completely autonomous congregations. The glue that held the SBC together was a shared focus on missions and evangelism, plus the creation, oversight, partial funding, and other support of a variety of SBC institutions.

During the past two decades, however, several leaders have contended that the SBC should be transformed into a church with a clearly worded doctrinal statement. That issue has evolved into a highly divisive internal quarrel. The quarrel has reached the stage that some are asking, "When do you believe our denomination will split?" An increasingly frequent response is "It already has."

As was pointed out earlier, while the United Church of Christ identifies itself as a "church," their constitution makes it clear it really is a voluntary association of completely autonomous congregations, plus dozens of independent conferences and other agencies. One consequence is, the UCC must utilize a different system for raising money than is used in the Roman Catholic, Episcopal, or United Methodist systems.

Do you believe a religious body must have a broadly agreed-upon belief statement or doctrine to call itself a church? Presbyterians, Episcopalians, Roman Catholics, and United Methodists go a step beyond that. The constitution of The United Methodist Church, like those of the other three religious bodies, requires agreement on both doctrine and polity. Others, however, require agreement only on a simple and fairly inclusive doctrinal statement and affirm congregational self-determination on polity.

If the time has come to reinvent The United Methodist Church for the twenty-first century, should it be designed as a church with a precisely stated doctrinal stance and a polity based on uniformity? Or, should it be reinvented as an association of congregations with a broadly defined, shared Wesleyan heritage, but a high degree of self-determination in both doctrine and polity? Or uniformity in polity, but self-determination in doctrine? (From this observer's perspective the clock has run out on the option of uniformity in doctrine. That is why @ *Risk* is such an important and timely book! That debate has moved from a focus on doctrine to a conflict over control.)

One of several alternatives would be for The United Methodist Church to reinvent itself with a traditional Christian doctrinal statement and as a federation of nongeographical affinity conferences. The glue that would hold this confederation together would include that shared doctrinal statement that would be a required component of the constitution of every conference and congregation; a common commitment to evangelism; a shared approach to global missions; a design to encourage congregations to learn from one another how to do church in twenty-first–century America; and a clear commitment to the need for each conference to design its own customized ministry plan and the organizational structure required to implement that plan. That should qualify the successor body to be described as a church.

On the one hand that would represent a compromise between the Roman Catholic and Anglican heritage, and on the other hand the American demand for the right of self-determination. Do you believe the supporters of this or a similar compromise would outnumber the opponents? Or, do you believe the folks who either are indifferent or in denial constitute the real majority in this denomination today? The ship could be sinking while everyone gathers to enjoy one another's company and what turns out to be their last meal together.

One of the critical issues is, Who controls the criteria for approving candidates for ordination? Are these candidates required to affirm and support a uniform denomination-wide statement of faith? Or, can each congregation define the criteria for the examination of candidates who will be ordained by and in that congregation? In the successor to the UMC will the denomination examine and ordain? Will one doctrinal statement be used throughout the denomination? Or, will the successor be an association of congregations with complete local autonomy on doctrinal positions? Or, will a simple majority determine the doctrinal position for all? Or, will each conference define its own requirements for ordination?

The Universalist Unitarian Association (UUA) is a contemporary example of an association of congregations. Currently, the desire for harmony and unity requires leaders in the UUA to avoid any discussion about the existence of a Supreme Being.

How Big?

In terms of congregations, The United Methodist Church is the second largest religious body in North America. If the number of constituents or the average weekend worship attendance is used to measure size, the UMC is the third largest. During the past ninety-five years this denomination and its predecessors have eliminated two congregations for every new one—and that ratio may be closer to 5 to 2. (Hundreds of new missions either died or were disbanded before they could be organized.) Given the fact the population of the United States more than tripled during those nine and one-half decades, do those ratios suggest this is a dysfunctional system? Or, do those ratios suggest this denomination is too large to be managed effectively? Or, do those ratios suggest there is no one in charge? Or, are those ratios a product of intentional decisions by the policymakers to withdraw from the American church scene?

Another perspective in this discussion of the future of the UMC can be gained by looking at those crucial distinctions between numerically growing institutions, and those that are shrinking in numbers; between winners and losers; between those institutions that generate loyalty, and those that create alienation; and between those that motivate members to rally together in reaching a common goal, and those that generate internal conflict.

The first point has been discussed earlier. The covenant community follows a different rule book than is appropriate for a voluntary association. Which rule book do you believe should guide the design for a strategy for this branch of American Methodism in the twenty-first century? Which rule book do you believe will produce the desired outcomes?

A second point comes in the form of a question: Why has divisive intradenominational quarreling been expanding in scope and growing in intensity during the past four decades? One part of the short answer is that gradual evolution from a covenant community into a voluntary association. The other part is the ecological context, or the behavior setting. The institutional organization and culture are now supportive of open intradenominational quarreling.

A longer historical discussion takes us back to the 1920s and 1930s. Between 1926 and 1936 the predecessor denominations experienced a decrease of 15,000 in the number of congregations and a drop of over 1 million in the combined membership. The quarrels of that era included the terms of the denominational reunions of 1922 and 1939; fundamentalism; the future of German language congregations and nationality conferences; sanctification; the candidacy of a Roman Catholic for president of the United States; the financial support of church-sponsored institutions; the repeal of prohibition, Darwinism, neo-orthodoxy. Intradenominational quarreling, numerical decline, and a shortage of dollars appeared to be compatible trends for this branch of American Methodism in the 1920s and 1930s.

The 1940s and 1950s were marked nationally by patriotism, prosperity, national unity, and an increase in church attendance. The Methodist Church enjoyed a rise in congregational receipts, a decline in intradenominational quarreling, a new burst of activity in new church development, a remarkable increase in designated contributions for benevolences, and a flood of candidates for the ordained ministry. The two predecessor denominations set a new record for combined membership in 1964. The combined average Sunday school attendance peaked as well—over 4 million in the early 1960s. Do you believe that was a coincidence? Or, do you see a possible correlation between internal harmony and numerical growth?

If the focus is shifted to the seven largest Christian bodies in the United States that trace their origins back to before 1850, what do they share as common characteristics? All seven (UMC, SBC, ELCA, PCUSA, Roman Catholic, Lutheran Church-Missouri Synod, and Episcopal) report the increase in their average worship attendance in recent years has been slower than the increase in the population of the United States. All seven also have been engaged in disruptive and divisive internal conflict in recent years. Are those two common characteristics simply a coincidence? Or, do they represent a predictable pattern in aging institutions? Or, are they a product of size? Or, are they a consequence of the rise in competition for future constituents? Or, are those two patterns a natural, normal, and predictable consequence of the recent growth of individualism in the American culture? A brief detour will introduce some research that may shed valuable light on this question.

Forty years ago the Stanford University Press published an extraordinarily significant, and widely ignored, research report. This book summarized a series of studies on "the effects of group and institutional size upon the behavior of children."[8] While the authors were reluctant to recommend a precise number as the ideal size for a four-year public high school, they published a number of guiding generalizations. For example, the proportion of students engaged in extracurricular activities begins to decrease when the total enrollment passes 150. Undesirable behavior patterns among the students increase as size goes up. Academic performance tends to go down, and the dropout rate goes up as size increases. This book and literally thousands of subsequent research reports have demonstrated that institutions can and should be perceived as "behavior settings." The design of each behavior influences how the participants respond in many different ways.

One recent response in educational circles has been the creation of a movement to encourage the organization of more small high schools. The Bill and Melinda Gates Foundation has made tens of millions of dollars in grants to increase the number of small high schools.

On the American ecclesiastical landscape we encounter relatively little intradenominational quarreling within those religious traditions that include fewer than 2,000 congregations. One reason may be they tend to be able to keep ministry, missions, and evangelism at the top of their agenda. One reason they are able to do that is they are relatively small institutions.

With approximately 35,000 congregations, do you believe The United Methodist Church is too small, the right size, or too large? If you conclude it includes too many congregations, do you believe the most productive response to this issue of size is to continue cutting back on the number of congregations and members? Or, do you believe the time may be coming to consider dividing this huge denomination into perhaps five or six smaller denominations.

Shaping a Strategy for the Future

We have now reached the point in this chapter at which we can confront a guaranteed trend. During the next six decades all the current members of The United Methodist Church who were born before 1960 will choose one of three paths: (1) switch to another religious tradition, (2) drop out of church completely, or (3) die. Some will choose all three.

What should be UMC strategy for attracting new constituents born after 1960? Here is a small package of questions that demand attention. Your responses to these questions will influence the design of the strategy that will earn your support.

A hundred years ago the six predecessor denominations included a combined total of nearly 57,000 congregations. The vast majority served a constituency living within three miles of the meeting place. One consequence was thousands of Methodist churches located approximately six miles from another Methodist church. In many cities, however, because of differing denominational affiliations, the distance between buildings could be measured in feet or blocks. An Evangelical Church, a Methodist Episcopal Church, and a Methodist Protestant Church might be located in the same block. That was not a problem! The vast majority of Americans walked to work, to school, to the post office, to the grocery store, to the lodge hall, to the doctor's office, to friends' houses, or to church.

The small neighborhood church continues to be the favorite of American churchgoers born before 1910, but the majority of American churchgoers born after 1960 appear to be comfortable riding in a privately owned motor vehicle to work, to the supermarket, to the medical clinic, to the motion picture theater, to the ballgame, to socials with friends or relatives, to school, or to a large regional church.

What do you believe? Should the ministry plan for this denomination for the twenty-first century continue the operational policies of the past three decades of increasing the number of congregations averaging 34 or fewer at worship, while sharply decreasing the number averaging 35 or more?

A persuasive argument can be made that the natural size of a worshiping community in American Protestantism averages between 15 and 40 at worship, but few of these can either financially afford or vocationally challenge a full-time seminary trained elder. They are, however, operationally viable. Combine a meeting place constructed and paid for by earlier generations of members, with a trained team of three to seven volunteers for leading worship, plus a sermon chosen by that team and delivered by videotape, plus a team of three volunteer caregivers trained by the Stephen Ministries, plus an adult *Alpha* and/or *Disciple* Bible study class led by a trained volunteer, plus a licensed sacramentalist, and the need for a resident pastor is eliminated.

Do you believe that should be a large component of the UM ministry plan for the twenty-first century? Or, do you believe the small lay-led house is a better option for perpetuating the small-church orientation of this denomination? Or, do you believe the number-one variable should be to provide full-time jobs for seminary graduates? There is an emerging consensus in American Protestantism that if the goal is to provide a challenging assignment to a full-time seminary graduate, an average worship attendance of 125 to 135 or more is required. Only 1 out of 5 UM congregations fits in that size bracket.

If, however, you believe that a high priority should be placed on the dissolution or merger of those 21,000 UM congregations averaging fewer than 75 at worship, you may advocate a greater reliance on circuits. These call for one minister to serve concurrently as the pastor of two or more small congregations. This has been a far more useful tactic for closing or merging congregations than for attracting younger generations of churchgoers. It also has been a way to distribute those surplus dollars in the conference treasury for subsidies.

Or, do you believe that the younger generations of American churchgoers can be found in disproportionately large numbers in the regional congregations averaging 500 or more at worship? That appears to be the minimum size required for a congregation to be able to mobilize the resources needed to offer the quality, relevance, and choices these younger generations expect from church. Here we see two different operational policies within the same denomination. As was pointed out in chapter 1, most of the annual conferences in the south central and southeastern jurisdictions have decided to increase the number of large congregations. In the other three jurisdictions most of the conferences have implemented operational policies consistent with shrinking the number of large UM congregations. Which outcomes do you favor?

One consequence of choosing the large regional church option can be illustrated by a pair of numbers. The small neighborhood church may draw most of its constituents from within a three-mile radius. The large regional congregation typically attracts people from a ten- to fifteen-mile radius. What's the difference? One obvious difference is the size of the church-owned parking lot. Will it accommodate 30 motor vehicles or 300? Or 700? Or 1,500?

A less obvious but far more significant difference can be summarized in one word—competition.[9] The service area of that congregation attracting people from a ten-mile radius is eleven times the size of the service area of the congregation drawing constituents from within a three-mile radius of the meeting place. One consequence is that large regional church probably has to compete with five to fifteen times as many other churches for prospective future constituents as does that small neighborhood church. One alternative for that small church is to carve out a distinctive niche in a larger service area. It might, for example, specialize in reaching couples in a bicultural marriage, or it could specialize in challenging and equipping childless adults—both married and single and who were born after 1965—to be engaged in doing ministry as lay volunteers. That small church, however, will not be able to compete with those large regional congregations in terms of quality and choices.

What do you believe should be the higher priority in building ministries with the generations born after 1960? To encourage the emergence of more very large regional congregations that can compete with that growing number of megachurches? Or, do you believe a more appropriate priority would be to encourage small UM churches to define and fulfill a distinctive specialized niche?

What do you believe is the largest source of new constituents for most congregations in contemporary American Protestantism? The children of members? Nonbelievers who become new converts to Christianity? This traveler's experiences suggest the largest source consists of baptized self-identified believers searching for a new church home. Many are in the process of searching and switching but have not changed their place of residence. Others are believers who are newcomers to that community.

Which of these three alternatives do you believe these church shoppers will choose? A congregation affiliated with a denomination polarized over several divisive issues? A congregation

affiliated with a denomination unified around a focus on evangelism and missions? Or a nondenominational congregation?

The last of this series of overlapping questions is generated by
the current intradenominational quarrel between the migrants
from Athens and those from Jerusalem. One perspective for
describing the differences between those two parties is the difference between ambiguity and certainty. The folks from
Athens tend to be more comfortable with considerable ambiguity in defining the core beliefs of the Christian faith. The
migrants from Jerusalem clearly are more comfortable articulat-
ing with a high degree of certainty: "This is what we believe,
this is what we teach, and this is why we do what we do in our
ministry."

Both parties in contemporary American Protestantism actually
display a relatively high degree of latitude, especially when compared to a hundred years ago, in scores of practices. That long list
includes divorce and remarriage after divorce; observance of the
Sabbath, the day of the week when that congregation gathers
people together for the corporate worship of God; attendance at
motion picture theaters; worshiping with a congregation from a
different Christian tradition; which translation of the Bible will
be used in worship; the role of women in the church; the use of
modern technology such as indoor plumbing and the use of projected visual imagery on a screen; the requirements for ordination; the reliance on donor-directed second-mile giving; the
appropriate attire for those leading and attending worship;
whether men and women will be permitted to sit next to one
another in worship; the appropriate housing for the pastor; issues
of human sexuality; couples living together before marriage; the
operation of Christian day schools; the choice of music for the
worship of God; and coed adult classes.

As The United Methodist Church designs a ministry plan for
reaching younger generations, do you believe the top priority
should be on reaching the folk from Athens or those from
Jerusalem? Or, do you believe this denomination can and should
attempt to reach and serve both of those constituencies? Or, are
you concerned that the present system may be so dysfunctional

that it will be impossible to design and implement an internally coherent and consistent strategy?

Is It a Dysfunctional System?

One widely accepted fact of organizational life today is that W. Edwards Deming was right.[10] Systems do produce the outcomes they are designed to produce. That is an accepted beginning point by reformers seeking to reduce the number of unnecessary deaths among hospital patients, among managers seeking to reduce defects in the manufacture of motor vehicles, and among educators who want to reduce the level of boredom among sixteen-year-old males in that very large public high school.

One definition of a dysfunctional system is that despite the continued supply of inputs (people's time, energy, creativity, money, real estate, and so forth) into one end of that system, the outcomes do not match what is desired. Do you believe that organization called The United Methodist Church is a dysfunctional system? That is a tough call! To answer that question one needs to identify the widely desired outcomes the UMC system is expected to produce. In the absence of an annual performance audit of each congregation, district, annual conference, and national agency, it is impossible to clearly compare the actual outcomes with the desired outcomes. One exception is most of the districts, annual conferences, and national agencies expect that shrinking number of congregations to send more dollars to headquarters every year.

It is relatively easy to identify dozens of actual outcomes produced by this system during the past few decades. That long list includes the shrinking of the ice cube described in the first chapter; fewer career overseas missionaries; an aging of the membership; an increase in the level of intradenominational quarreling; a withdrawal from the large central cities and older suburbs across the North; a sharp reduction of $600 million in the unfunded liability of the pension system between 1982 and 2001 (the unfunded liability did increase by $137 million between January 1,

2002 and January 2, 2003); an increase in the number of very large congregations in the South and Southwest; an increase in the number of bishops and district superintendents who are female and/or come from an African or Asian or Latino ancestry; the emergence of several self-identified UM teaching churches; an increase in the proportion of newly ordained elders who are not graduates of UM seminaries; a reduction in the number of congregations averaging 100 to 350 at worship; an increase in the number of congregations who turn to non-UMC agencies to purchase resources; an increase in the number of UM ministers with an earned doctorate; a reduction in the number of delegates to the General Conference from persons living in the North and West; an increase in the number of ordained ministers of Korean ancestry; an increase in the number of congregations with an endowment or trust fund; an increase in the number of dollars received by the World Service Fund; an increase in the number of congregations reporting an average worship attendance of 10 or fewer; and the dissolution or merger of several thousand congregations.

If one of the most desired outcomes is the transformation of the lives of adults born before 1970, a big success story can be found among the thousands of adult United Methodists who have been engaged as short-term volunteer missionaries in doing ministry with fellow Christians in a sister church on another continent. Most of the volunteers in those teams of seven to thirty churchgoers return as transformed Christians![11] The tough question is to define which of these and other actual outcomes were intentionally sought by those who operate the system. An even more difficult question is to identify who has both the authority and the responsibility to describe the desired outcomes and to operate the system.

Another description of a dysfunctional system is the one that adopted a clearly written rulebook to guide the players in a game called "Spreading Scriptural Holiness Across the Land." Two centuries later that game has evolved into a quarrel over who will be the umpire to interpret the rulebook.

A definition of a dysfunctional religious system could be one that schedules a national convention once every three or four years. One of the top priorities on the agenda is a proposal to persuade the constituents to increase their level of giving to the national headquarters. A second agenda item, which is guaranteed to produce far more publicity in the secular press, is to persuade the delegates to choose sides on a polarizing issue such as homosexuality. Will the losers on this second issue return home and aggressively urge their fellow parishioners to contribute more money to national denominational agencies and causes?

A common description of a dysfunctional system is one in which means-to-an-end concerns have replaced the original purpose in determining the priorities for the allocation of scarce resources.

Do you believe The United Methodist Church has become a dysfunctional system?

Is Schism Inevitable?

What do you believe the next dozen years will bring to The United Methodist Church? First, do you believe the combination of denial, an increase in apportionments for the national agencies to approximately $600 million for the 2005–2008 quadrennium, a strong attachment to "How we've always done things in the UMC," and continued refusal to build in a better system of accountability will increase the level of detachment (or alienation) between the people in the pews and the denominational system? Or, do you believe that line in the sand will be smoothed over during the next few years?

Second, when you study the globe, where do you believe the greatest increase in UM membership will take place? Will the net increase be found largely in the southeastern and south central jurisdictions in the United States and the Central Conferences on other continents? That has been the pattern for the past three or four decades. Or, do you believe the big increases in UM membership will be found in the other three jurisdictions in the United States?

Third, what do you believe will be the most significant points of commonality in those conferences, both U.S. and overseas, that will be reporting net increases in membership in the coming years? While many exceptions do exist, in broad general terms, currently that list includes points of commonality on biblical interpretation, the priority given to evangelism, the definition of the parish ministry as a calling rather than as a profession, on a variety of social and political issues, and on the importance of planting new missions.

In summary, do you believe a growing number of UM members from Jerusalem and a shrinking number from Athens will have found a way to live together in peace and harmony by 2015? Or, do you believe they will have chosen schism over continuing those intradenominational quarrels?

How Do You Measure a Turnaround?

It is not unreasonable to expect that the fourth great religious revival in American history, which began back in the 1960s, will combine with that recent increase in the number of large UM congregations to produce a reversal of the numerical decline of the 1960–2000 era. For example, in 2006, when the statistical reports for 2005 will have been tabulated, a summary could resemble this statement:

"For the five years since the end of 2000, the full membership of The United Methodist Church in the United States increased from 8.34 million to 8.7 million. Baptisms (all ages) rose from 150,690 to 161,000. The number of persons on the preparatory membership rolls climbed from 1,325,270 to slightly over 1,480,000. Average worship attendance grew from that plateau of 3.49 million to 3.69 million in 2005, the highest since 1972. The grand total for congregational expenditures passed $6.1 billion for the first time in history in 2004 and was nearly $6.4 billion for 2005, compared to less than $4.8 billion back in 2000. Total benevolences came to slightly over $6.2 million in 2005, another new record, and up from $481 million in 2000."

Do you believe that a rising tide will lift all the ships in the UM harbor? Or only a few?

One way to obtain a quick appraisal on a conference-by-conference basis could be to sort out the 5 percent of congregations that reported the greatest numerical growth in average worship attendance from the end of 2000 to the end of 2005. What was their combined net increase in their average worship attendance for that five-year period? How does that number compare to the combined net increase in average worship attendance for the other 95 percent of the congregations in that annual conference? This observer predicts that in one-half of the conferences that increase by that 5 percent will exceed the combined increase of the other 95 percent. In the remaining conferences that combined total for the 5 percent will be a plus figure, while the net figure for the other 95 percent will be a minus number.

What do you expect will be the pattern for this 2001–2005 period? If the trend in your annual conference resembles either of these two patterns, how will you interpret it?

How Urgent?

How soon do you believe action should be taken to resolve some of the issues identified in this book? Perhaps the most unrealistic is to hope the General Conference of 2004 will act on at least two or three of what the delegates agree are the most urgent issues. Why is that unrealistic? One reason, of course, is time. A couple of weeks in the spring in Pennsylvania provides too little time. A more crucial factor, however, is that in many of the annual conferences the processes to elect the delegates were to be used if the central goal was not to generate broad-based agreement but rather to deepen the polarization within the constituency.

A second alternative would be to schedule a special session of the General Conference for 2006 and to appoint a fifteen-member special commission to prepare an agenda for that session. Ideally, that commission would be able to agree on the three to five most urgent issues to be addressed. One of the top priorities for that short agenda should be to address that growing disengagement between congregational leaders and the denominational agencies. One source of that disengagement is the absence of an effective system of accountability. This is an especially urgent issue in the current budgeting processes for both the annual conferences and the national agencies.

In preparing its recommendations, that commission also would offer the delegates two choices on each proposed course of action for each issue. The delegates would be required to choose between Change A and Change B. Perpetuating the status quo by not approving any changes would not be offered as an option. The time to argue has been replaced by the time to act.

Do you believe the General Conference can adopt a strategy for this denomination for the twenty-first century? Or, do you believe each annual conference should design and implement its own customized strategy? Or, do you believe that the most the General Conference can be expected to do is to raise apportionments and, perhaps, adopt enabling legislation that would challenge self-identified groups of congregations to come together and design their own customized strategy?

Another alternative would be to postpone any serious remedial proposals until 2008. One price tag on that probably would be a rise in that level of disengagement. One benefit would be four additional years for those addicted to intradenominational quarreling. While the constituency probably will continue to grow older in age and fewer in numbers in the North and West, the decreased rate of institutional decline for the denomination as a whole probably will comfort those who prefer denial over change.

It also is possible that by 2008 the United States Congress will adopt some form of universal health insurance that will alleviate that problem. The big uncertainties on that are (1) will it happen by 2008; (2) will it be funded by income taxes, excise taxes, or by a tax on employers (if the funding is a tax on the employer, will the congregation or the annual conference be defined as the employer?); and (3) will it cover all costs for health care or will each recipient be required to pay part of the costs?

Likewise, by the spring of 2008 it may be possible to determine whether that UM ice cube is continuing to melt. If the melting has been halted, it may be possible to identify and export to other denominations what have turned out to be the most productive turnaround strategies in this branch of American Methodism.

Why not postpone any action until 2012?

From this observer's experience, it is easier and more productive to plan from strength than from weakness. Equally important, by 2012 the coming crisis in financing Social Security payments (which are based on intergenerational transfer of income) and Medicare will have begun to dominate the national political scene. It also is possible that by 2012 schism will have replaced institutional reform as the most attractive option.

How urgent do you believe the need is for constructive action? Before answering that question, you may want to look at a half dozen other perspectives on this subject.

CHAPTER FOUR

SIX OTHER PERSPECTIVES

W hy is a chapter on other perspectives needed for this
book? That question requires a few autobiographical
comments. First, and most obvious, is I am an old
man. Therefore we need the perspective of younger women.
(That inventory is far larger than the number of UM women who
are older than this writer!) Second, as has been stated repeatedly,
the motivation for writing this book came from reading @ *Risk*.
Since I do not have the qualifications required to write from that
perspective, I hoped to secure two essays from people who are
qualified to do that. In response to my invitations I received two
gentle, thoughtful, and clearly articulated essays. One is from a
UM clergywoman and the other from a UM clergyman.

A third personal handicap is I am an ordained minister. While
I was an active layman in a large central city congregation before

enrolling in seminary, that was in another era on another planet in another galaxy where American Methodists were united and relatively young, and that system was producing desired outcomes. Therefore I placed a high priority on securing the perspective of an informed active and thoughtful layperson who also is a delegate to General Conference in 2004 and who brings highly relevant professional competencies to this assignment. That explains why his essay is the second one in this chapter.

Among my most valuable and relevant personal qualifications for writing this book is that in 1986 I was diagnosed with cancer of the colon. Thanks to the skills and persistence of a scientist, who was my primary care physician at that time, plus early detection, the miracles of modern medicine, and two rounds of surgery in four days (thanks to a pathologist who erred the first time but quickly corrected that error), I am a survivor!

Cancer survivors tend to be optimists. I continue to be optimistic about the potential of my beloved United Methodist Church for ministry in the twenty-first century. Early detection of malfunctions in the system, plus a willingness to admit and seek to correct errors are foundation stones for building a better future in any large and complex system.

Fairness requires that readers of this book should know that none of the other contributors to this chapter had the opportunity to read the other six chapters in this book before writing their essay. Each was mailed a relatively small section relevant to their theme, but deadlines made it impossible for them to read the rest of this manuscript. That September 26, 2003, deadline applied to everyone, including this writer.

The book @ *Risk* introduces the reader to a deep and noisy quarrel among United Methodists today. That is true. One of my differences with the book, however, is I am convinced that loud intradenominational quarrel is but one of several undesirable outcomes of a dysfunctional system. Therefore we need to look at several other undesirable outcomes; but is there still time to do that? One reason I believe there is still time is that in June 1998 I was diagnosed with kidney failure. I learned how to live on dialysis for several weeks. I learned how to be unbelievably grateful when I was able to go off dialysis. I also learned that what clearly was a last-minute diagnosis can be useful in creating a new future. Therefore, while the United Methodist ice cube continues to melt, I continue to be optimistic about what the future could bring, given an accurate diagnosis and the appropriate therapy.

While one of my handicaps may be a surplus of optimism, I do realize the value of soliciting the views of others who bring a background and a perspective I have not earned. Since I am not a scholar, I sought a scholar and a seminary professor who could and would add that dimension to this chapter. She has met that urgent deadline.

Another one of my hundreds of limitations is I have never served as the senior minister of a megachurch. Combine that fact with my conviction that one of the most significant differences between the annual conferences in the North and West and those in the South is about the future. The operational policies, whether intentional or not, of many annual conferences in the North appear to be designed to increase the number of small congregations and decrease the number of large UM churches. By contrast, the operational policies of several annual conferences in the South appear to be designed to increase the number of large churches. Table B in chapter 1 documents that observation. Do you believe the future of American Protestantism will bring an increase in the number of small and midsized churches? Or, do you agree with this observer that a disproportionately large number of the American churchgoers born after 1960 apparently prefer large churches? Do you believe the generations born after 1960 will outlive those born before 1950? Those two questions led me to invite the founding pastor of a very large UM congregation in the Southwest to contribute an essay to this chapter.

Finally, I am convinced that the many lines in the UM sand described in chapter 2, and the melting of that UM ice cube are not the real problems. The real problem is they are the undesired outcomes of a dysfunctional system. One of the characteristics of a dysfunctional system is it often turns nice innocent people into victims. Combine that unfortunate fact of life with the conviction that the most widely neglected facet of this dysfunctional system is an inequitable, unfair, and underfunded system for retirement benefits for retired pastors. To introduce that essay, we need to take a trip down memory lane with two fictional couples.

Mark & Mary and Carl & Cathy

Mark Mitchell was born on a farm in April 1932. The oldest of three children, Mark combined school and farm work as he grew into manhood, but he decided against farming as a career. A month before his eighteenth birthday in 1950, he received the letter accepting his application to begin school the following September at the state university. Two weeks later his father suddenly died of a heart attack. Mark canceled his plans to go away to school and spent the next three years helping his mother run the farm and rear the two younger children. He became very active in that small open-country Methodist church. In 1952 he felt a call to the ministry. He and his mother agreed that the following year, when Mark's brother graduated from high school, that son could replace Mark on the farm, and Mark could enroll in college. Thus in September 1953 that twenty-one-year-old pre-seminary student enrolled in a small Methodist college.

Within weeks Mark met and soon became close friends with another twenty-one-year-old freshman, Carl Cook. Carl had graduated from high school in 1950. Immediately after the outbreak of war in Korea, Carl, the middle child in a family with three sons and two daughters, enlisted in the United States Army. While in Korea he became a close friend of a Methodist chaplain. Carl decided the ministry was his calling. When he was discharged in the summer of 1953, he enrolled in that same Methodist college Mark had selected.

The extroverted and gregarious Carl made friends very easily; but by March 1954 he began to focus his affections on another first-year student, Cathy Owens. Cathy was, by four minutes, the older of twin sisters. In early May, Carl set his buddy Mark up with a blind date with Cathy's twin sister, Mary. To make a long story short, in late May 1957, all four graduated from college. A week later, two weddings were held in a Methodist church, as Mark and Mary were united in the bonds of holy matrimony thirty minutes after Carl and Cathy were married. That summer Mark and Carl worked in construction jobs to save money for seminary.

In September Mark and Carl enrolled in seminary. Mary found a job teaching in an elementary school, and Cathy worked as a teller in a bank. They lived in a small apartment building for married students that the seminary had constructed in 1948. Carl enjoyed a veteran's educational benefits; Mary's salary was larger than Cathy's. Mark and Carl were both in a hurry to graduate, so they went to summer school in 1958 and 1959, carried above-average classroom loads, and graduated in January 1960.

At this point their career paths took them down different roads. Mark was invited to become the third of three ministers on the staff of a large university church in an annual conference that now is largely urban and suburban. Carl chose an annual conference that was predominantly rural and small-town. For the first time in their lives, the twin sisters found themselves living eight hundred miles apart, but the two couples did visit each other during vacations. Each couple was blessed with three healthy children, all of whom graduated from college.

During the next forty years, Carl served eight appointments: a three-point circuit, another three-point circuit, a two-point circuit, a small-town church, a second small-town church, a third small-town church, a county-seat town church, and a larger county-seat church that averaged 175 at worship. That was Carl's first and only experience with paid program staff. He had a part-time minister of music, a part-time director of Christian education, and a part-time seminary student during his last three years before retirement. On their retirement Carl and Cathy boasted, "We have lived in eight different parsonages, and we left each one in better shape than it was when we moved there." Carl's on-the-job training polished his amateur skills as a carpenter, painter, mason, electrician, and plumber.

Mark's ministerial career included only three appointments. The first was that superb learning experience for eight years on the staff of the university church. That was followed by twelve years as the second pastor of a new mission founded in 1948. When Mark arrived in 1968, worship attendance was averaging 145. By the time he left in 1980, that congregation had relocated from the original one-acre site to a twelve-acre parcel of land, had constructed and paid for new physical facilities, and was averaging 685 at worship. Mark's third and last appointment was as the senior minister of the largest congregation in that annual conference. Founded in 1951, it was averaging 750 at worship the year before Mark arrived, and 1,240 in 1999, the year before Mark retired.

In Mark's third year, the church-owned parsonage was razed and replaced by a two-story classroom building, and Mark was given a housing allowance. Mark and Mary purchased a new house for $165,000 in 1983 and paid for it with their tax-exempt housing allowance in a fifteen-year mortgage.

In the summer of 2000 these two 68-year-old Methodist ministers retired. Each was the oldest in his retirement class that year. Later each one commented, "The majority of the ministers who retired the year I did were under 65 years of age." Both Mark and Carl said to their wives back in 1999, "Honey, for nearly forty years, you have faithfully and lovingly told me, 'Wherever the Lord calls you to go, I will follow.' Now it's your turn. You tell me where you want to live in retirement, and I will follow you."

Mary and Cathy had anticipated this and had agreed on an answer. "We want to live out the rest of our lives in the sun next door to each other." Mark and Carl happily agreed. Thanks to the booming housing market, Mark and Mary sold their house for $345,000. Thanks to the combination of a thrifty lifestyle and the fact that Cathy had worked full-time during five of Carl's eight appointments, they had accumulated $63,000 in certificates of deposit.

The two couples spent the summer and fall of 2000 looking for the right community in which to retire. In November 2000 they found their dream location. They also found two nearly identical single-family houses next door to each other that had been built in 1992 and were for sale by widows—one for $160,000, and the other for $165,000. Mark and Mary paid cash for theirs and still had nearly $300,000 in investments. Carl and Cathy purchased the other with a $50,000 down payment and a $110,000 mortgage. The good news was the monthly payments on their ten-year mortgage, property taxes, utilities, and insurance were all income deductible from their monthly pension checks as housing allowance expenditures.

In April 2002 the seventy-year-old Mark, like his father years earlier, died of a sudden heart attack. Four months later, a drunken and uninsured twenty-year-old driver with an expired driver's license went through a red traffic signal and killed himself and Carl. That accident occurred as Carl was on his way home. He had just completed the interview and was immediately offered a job in a superstore specializing in home remodeling supplies. The combination of Carl's forty years renovating parsonages, plus his perpetual warm smile and the reassurance offered by his grandfatherly appearance, had made him the ideal candidate to fill that vacancy in customer service.

As you read this, these twin sisters are sitting in the sun. Each one is the widow of a United Methodist minister who served more than forty years as a parish pastor. Each one faithfully followed her husband from one appointment to another. Both are in excellent health. The mortality tables suggest each has a probable life expectancy of at least fifteen or sixteen more years. They enjoy each other's company. Cathy now has five grandchildren, and Mary has four.

What's the difference between these two widows?

Mary lives in a paid-for house. She taught for a total of twenty-two years in the public schools in the same state, and now enjoys a generous teacher's pension. Those Social Security checks, and the monthly pension checks from The United Methodist Church General Board of Pension and Health Benefits are smaller than they were before Mark's death, but the $15,000 annual income from an annuity fund she purchased after Mark's death continues. She is covered by Medicare, and Mark's annual conference provides generous supplemental coverage for a monthly payment of only $50 by Mary.

Cathy still has several years to go in meeting those monthly mortgage payments, plus insurance, property taxes, and utility bills. Since Carl's death, none of these can be deducted from her income as a housing allowance. In Carl's annual conference, the past-service rate for the years Carl served as a pastor before 1982 is a shade above one-half what it is in Mark's conference. That means Cathy's monthly pension checks are significantly lower than the amount received by her twin sister. Cathy never lived in one place long enough to hold a job where she could build up a vested interest in a pension account, so she receives nothing similar to Mary's teacher's pension. Nearly all the savings Carl and Cathy had accumulated before retirement went into the down payment in that house, so she has no investment income. Because of the difference in the payments into Social Security by Carl and the highly paid Mark, Cathy's Social Security check is for a smaller amount. Last year Carl's annual conference decided it no longer was economically possible to provide supplemental health insurance, even for a fee, to survivors of retired ministers. The current big issue in that annual conference, which has experienced a 30 percent decrease in membership since 1960, is whether it will be possible to continue those annual increases in the past-service rate for the twenty-two years Carl served before 1982. Lest there be any misunderstanding, both of these widows are financially comfortable in their retirement years, but Mary's monthly income is more than twice Cathy's. Cathy's annual expenditures, however, for mortgage payments and health care greatly exceed Mary's.

The moral of this story of two mythical twin sisters is that a common outcome of dysfunctional systems is to treat some people unfairly. If, however, you are convinced the system has not treated Cathy fairly, turn your thoughts to the twenty-two-year-old woman who married a black Methodist preacher in 1960; he served as a parish pastor until retirement in 2000. He died in 2002. How is the system treating his sixty-five-year-old widow?

Those who prefer to focus the blame on individuals rather than a dysfunctional system can make a case that Cathy's dilemma is Carl's fault. If, back in 1987–1988, Carl had offered himself as a candidate for the episcopacy and had been elected, that would have guaranteed them a brighter financial future. That not only would have doubled his compensation, thus enabling him and Cathy to save more for their retirement years, it also would have provided him with a large pension check every month and far more generous health benefits for him and his surviving widow.

Now that you have read this far, you can see why the essay by Barbara Boigegrain must be placed first as we look at other perspectives on the future of The United Methodist Church in the United States.

Will Unfunded Plans Become Unfulfilled Promises?

by Barbara Boigegrain

The United Methodist Church is in debt up to its ears to its clergy population! This is due to unfunded pension promises as well as unfunded retiree health coverage that conferences are providing to clergy. While the dollars can be big, this is not necessarily a problem, as long as there are realistic plans against which progress is made to pay off the debt.

Clearly, our denomination desires to provide clergy support and practice good stewardship. Two concepts have revolved around the discussion of clergy benefit support. These concepts, spoken of with great passion but defined in a multitude of ways, are "equitable" and "adequate." I will define them here for purposes of clarity, knowing that many will disagree. *Equitable* means fair based upon both historical and current expectations and covenant relationship. This includes fairness across levels of compensation, across geographic locations, and across time. It does not mean "the same." *Adequate* means necessary for a reasonable lifestyle, with dignity, as Wesley stated, "enough for food, shelter and a little bit more." In the context of our twenty-first–century itinerating clergy structure, we need also to include housing support and health coverage. We hope that pension support allows, with some prudence, for considerable discretionary income over a period of retirement, for both the clergy and spouse.

I will use these concepts to examine the two pension programs that provide financial support to our clergy: the pre-'82 program and the Ministerial Pension Plan (MPP). The pre-'82 "defined benefit" pension plan allows no new participants since 1981; however, nearly every annual conference increases the Past Service Rate (PSR) that is paid per year of service to all retirees with pre-'82 service. The purpose for the increase is to ensure that these benefits continue to be updated as compared to average compensation. The pre-'82 plan operated like a floor plan in which a minimum benefit was promised, but individual accounts were created; these accounts participated in the earnings growth that otherwise would have accrued to the plan. Had it been a true defined benefit plan, it would have been fully funded (except for future increases) many years ago.

There is a three-fold difference in the past service rate among conferences, with some paying PSR's over $600 and others under $200. Thus in the final analysis we reveal a plan that lacks equity across conferences, appears inadequate when compared to MPP balances, and, until the recent creation of conference funding plans, challenges our understanding of faithful stewardship since there is an annual and unevenly distributed growing liability as conferences separately vote PSR increases.

In 1982, The United Methodist Church chose to remedy some of the ills of the pre-'82 plan by adopting the Ministerial Pension Plan. Although some chose different contribution bases, this plan is considered equitable, since the 11 percent or 12 percent contribution is fairly consistent across conferences. By design, it is an individualistic plan providing for capital accumulation over the last twenty years. The underlying investments have performed very well, fully participating in an unprecedented stock market that greatly raised account balances.

Participants in the Ministerial Pension Plan have been protected from the downturns in the market because of the nature of the underlying investment vehicle: the Diversified Investment Fund. This is a "reserve fund" in that it holds back some of the investment earnings during positive-growth years so that it can keep principal from declining. A reserve fund works well in positive markets but is not sustainable in long-term flat or downward markets or where distributions exceed contributions due to the aging of the retired population and/or fewer new entrants into the system. This is because over time the reserves are depleted and cannot sustain crediting earnings that the market does not support.

Of greatest concern to me under this plan is the adequacy of the benefits for surviving spouses. When the minister dies, the spouse receives a reduction in church pension benefit and a 50 percent reduction in Social Security benefits, and loses the income tax exclusion.

Finally, we must acknowledge the issue of *security* in this discourse. The value of our denomination's stake in retiree health care exceeded $2 billion in 2002, and it is growing exponentially. A benefit program that is subject to the market and is "pay as you go" is not secure. As faithful stewards, we must responsibly note these truths: the possibility of weaker economies in the future, the probability of fewer people contributing to the plan, and future generations of The United Methodist Church unable (or unwilling or simply too few in numbers) to shoulder what appears to be an overwhelming burden.

Consequently, it is imperative to provide clergy benefits support that is equitable, adequate, and secure, and in a manner consistent with good stewardship, and to develop a consistent funding plan! Our denomination's covenant with those who serve in our diverse ministry sites will remain at risk until we address all of these issues fully, faithfully, and reasonably and have plans to pay for what we promise.

Barbara Boigegrain was born into and reared in the Methodist Church. She is a wife and mother and serves as the General Secretary of the General Board of Pension and Health Benefits of The United Methodist Church.

✳ ✳ ✳ ✳ ✳

The System Can Work!

by Donald R. House

When my father, now a retired United Methodist minister, once delivered a sermon to our annual conference, he provided a simple but penetrating request—in spite of controversy among its members, love the church! I always have. I do today. My perspectives are influenced by my experience as a delegate to General Conference, as a board member of the General Council on Finance and Administration, as a member of a General Conference assigned task force, and as an economist.

Instead of one single group seeking control of the denomination, there are multiple groups seeking desired solutions or positions on a variety of issues by appealing to the uninformed for delegate votes. Total control of the denomination is not within any one group's grasp.

The processes of debating and voting at General Conference in both the legislative committees and the plenary are remarkably fair. Interest groups do not seek total control; instead, they seek favored legislation in their areas of interest. Beyond their areas of interest, they seem to have little or no influence at all. No single interest group has gained control over a broad range of issues.

The task force to which I was assigned sought changes in an established set of rules that had remained in place for forty years. Its proposed changes created financial winners and losers. Initially, there was significant resistance to change. However, with sufficient research, documentation, and explanation, the resistance lessened. Proposed changes gained support, even among some of the financial losers. No group was ever in control—it was simply a matter of placing the complete evidence before the delegates. The General Conference changed the rules, and the process worked like it should. After forty years, the denomination turned a corner!

Our church faces more challenges, but no one group is in total control. No one group seeks total control. The General Conference awaits sound recommendations, sufficiently supported with research, documentation, and explanation. Progress can be slow, but I believe in the process. It is a democratic process that allows good recommmendations to surface, to be debated, and to be adopted. There are struggles, to be sure, but those engaged in these struggles love the church. There remains a unifying bond among members that overcomes the struggles.

Our denomination is losing members in the midst of a growing population. Worship and Sunday school attendance are decreasing, and our congregations and clergy are aging. These trends are well known and have existed for many years. These are among our most difficult challenges. It is easy to conclude that these trends are a result of a dysfunctional system—one that is resistant to change. However, there are other lesser known, more optimistic trends.

Member financial support of our denomination is increasing. The typical pattern of a dysfunctional organization is decreasing financial support from its members. Decreasing financial support is not happening. Between

1974 and 1995, giving per member has tracked almost perfectly disposable personal income per capita across the population. Over these years, there is no evidence of weakening financial support among our members. Increases in per capita incomes across the population, which reflects the per capita incomes of our membership, have led to equal percentage increases in per member giving to the church. Decreasing financial support would be evidenced by income growth outstripping contribution growth. While this financial record is good, it gets better.

Between 1995 and 2001, things changed. Giving per member increased faster than per capita incomes. The average member contributed a greater percentage of income to the church—more than we have seen in over twenty years.

The 2004 General Conference represents only one of thousands of decision-making bodies within the denomination. However, it stands as the single voice for the denomination. It sets the rules within which all other decisions are made. The decisions to be made by this General Conference are important.

Over the past twenty or so years, the denomination may have placed less confidence in the General Conference and more confidence in the annual conferences and local churches for solutions. The budget for the General Conference, which funds the general agencies, task forces, and the operations of the General Conference itself, reflects a decreasing percentage of total available dollars within the denomination. The General Conference budget is a decreasing portion of the total pie. This is a movement away from centralization.

I have wondered whether the shrinking of this denomination is a result of deliberate choice or a result of a flawed budgeting process. After participating in forming the budget recommendation to the 2004 General Conference, I believe that the budgeting process has its repairable faults, but I am not convinced that the shrink-ing of the denomination is a consequence of these flaws. This trend appears to be the product of informed choice.

The representation of United Methodists within resident populations varies remarkably across the regions. Among some annual conferences, United Methodists represent over 6 percent of the population, and in other states United Methodists represent less than 1 percent of the population. Perhaps a single set of solutions to apply to all annual conferences will miss the mark. Perhaps the annual conferences and local churches are best posi-tioned to address these challenges. Yet, if new effective solutions require more of our constituents, the needed resources will be made available even if it requires a reversal of the funding trend.

So, in spite of our challenges, I remain optimistic. The love for the church binds us together despite our differ-ences in opinions and beliefs. We have shown an increasing capacity to financially support our churches. Our democratic system encourages the introduction of new ideas, with the necessary discussion and debate. Our denomination is capable of finding and implement-ing solutions.

Donald R. House served as delegate to the 1996 and 2000 General Conferences, having led the Texas Annual Conference Delegation in 2000. He will serve as a del-egate to the 2004 General Conference, leading the laity of the delegation. He currently serves on the General Council on Finance and Administration. He has served as pres-ident of the Texas Annual Conference's Council on Finance and Administration. He earned a PhD in economics from Texas A&M University, and has taught economics at Auburn University and Texas A&M University. He currently serves as president of RRC, Inc., an economics research/consulting firm located in Texas.

✳ ✳ ✳ ✳ ✳

Next we turn to two contributors who both share the perspec-tive of @ Risk, but they come from two different institutional settings.

Courage to Hear God's Answers

by Kathryn J. Johnson

We really shouldn't ask questions unless we are ready for honest answers. Questions like "Honey, do these pants make me look heavy?" or "Sweetie, can you tell I'm bald when I comb my hair like this?" strike fear in the heart of many a spouse. Do the questioners *really* want to know the answer?

Looking at the controversies currently tearing at the fabric of The United Methodist Church, I'm coming to the conclusion that we're asking the wrong questions. One of the reasons for this, I believe, is that we are afraid of the answers. Unless and until we ask the right questions, however, we will not find our way forward.

Questions making the rounds these days include

- Who is responsible for the polarization of the UMC?
- Isn't the real problem that those on the "right" and those on the "left" are tearing the church apart?
- Which side will win? Or, will the battle continue endlessly?
- Who is being most faithful? Most biblical?
- Is anybody thinking about the folk in the middle?

There is no shortage of opinions about who is responsible for the current mess. The "right" claims that the "left" is being unbiblical. The "left" claims the "right" is being unfaithful. The middle claims that the "right" and the "left" are both irresponsibly extreme. Everyone claims they are being Wesleyan!

When I became involved with the Information Project for United Methodists and the book *United Methodism @ Risk,* I was keenly aware of the differences between conservatives and progressives in the church. Through extensive reading and research, I learned even more about the fundamental ways in which our perspectives diverge.

As my knowledge increased about the Institute on Religion and Democracy (IRD), and the related conservative renewal groups in The United Methodist Church, my commitment to educating United Methodists about the goals and strategies of these groups grew stronger. My anger at the tactics employed by some within these groups increased as I better understood the ways in which they have torn down, rather than built up, our denomination.

At the same time a very disconcerting thing began to happen. As I reflected on what I was reading and hearing, I began to feel some empathy for conservative, evangelical United Methodists. Many of the conservative renewal groups began at a time when the leadership of the national church was decidedly liberal. They felt that as a minority their voice was not being heard. Whether that was the reality or not, that was their perception.

As those of us on the "left" observe the decided shift toward a more conservative church, we are suddenly faced with the reality that our voices may be marginalized in the same way that those on the "right" feel they have been marginalized. I began to see some similarities between those on the "right" and on the "left." Horrors! How could this be?

Among our similarities are

- a deep commitment to the gospel as we understand it
- a willingness to act on our convictions
- an evangelical zeal to share our beliefs with others
- a belief that our faith understanding should inform our political action in the world
- a deep frustration when our voices are not heard within the church and when our beliefs do not find expression in church policy and action

I still firmly believe that the IRD is in many ways "using" the church to further a neoconservative political agenda, and should be challenged and stopped. I have come to see, however, that the conservative renewal groups in our church are not solely fueled by the IRD. Several of them came into being before the IRD was founded in 1981. The founders of Good News, for example, were firmly committed to making a strong evangelical witness within the church from their start in 1967.

While I have a very different understanding of evangelism, I admit that in reading about these early years of Good News, I am struck by the commitment of its adherents. Dare I say that it reminds me of the fervor of those of us today who are committed to a church that fully includes sexual minorities in all aspects of its life?

To the extent that the conservative renewal groups within United Methodism work in concert with the IRD, and joint efforts are substantial, they need to be confronted. But confrontation alone will not shed light to illuminate the path or paths that will lead us out of the darkness in which the UMC currently finds itself.

To stand in God's light, I believe we must be willing to let our defenses down and face one another honestly and humbly, admitting our own shortcomings. We must confess that we have spent an inordinate amount of energy fighting one another, and ask forgiveness for the ways in which this has detracted from our ability to minister to a broken and hurting world.

We must continue to speak the truth to our brothers and sisters in the faith, even to the point of strongly disagreeing. But that truth must be spoken in love. Blaming, finger pointing, and demonizing will not bring us, or the people we serve, closer to God.

We must be willing to ask fundamental questions and be ready for honest answers.

- How can the UMC best embody God's love at this point in history?

- We say that the mission of the church is to "make disciples of Jesus Christ." Can people with widely different understandings of what this means co-exist in one denomination? Is it possible to have one national mission agency, given our differences?
- United Methodists differ in their beliefs concerning whether Jesus is the one and only way to know God. Can we produce denominational Sunday school curricula and other study materials to encompass these different perspectives?
- Within the UMC we differ in our beliefs as to whether Scripture is the primary source of revelation or the sole source of revelation. Likewise, we differ on whether particular traditional expressions of the Christian faith, such as the Apostle's Creed, are sufficient in this day and age. Is the chasm between us too deep to cross?
- We differ in our understanding of the compatibility of homosexuality with Christian teaching. Can those who believe that homosexuality is sinful accept being part of a church whose polity makes room for those who affirm homosexuality? Can those who affirm homosexuality remain in a church that definitively denounces it?

Creative tension and differences can lead to dialogue and growth. They can also lead to acrimonious infighting that clouds our vision and saps our energy. This is where we find ourselves today.

It's time to declare a cease-fire.

Do we have the courage to state our beliefs and convictions without needing to prove others wrong? Are we willing to do the hard work of identifying those things that are of core significance to our faith? Are we willing to compromise on matters that are not of core significance? Are we willing to face the possibility that our differences are such that we really can't remain within one denomination with integrity?

Personally, I am interested in exploring whether there are alternatives for the future of the church that we have not been able to see through the dust of the battlefield. Are there ways to configure our lives in the church that allow for the full expression of our differences while honoring our common heritage? Are there some ministries that we can hold in common while in others we diverge? If we discover that our differences truly are irreconcilable, and I fear this may be the case, how can we separate such that we leave each successor group whole?

It is my experience that God never leaves us without answers if we are willing to face the tough questions. I pray that we can love the church and the world enough to find the courage to listen for what God would have us do.

The Reverend Kathryn J. Johnson is an ordained elder in the New England Conference. She is the executive director of the Methodist Federation for Social Action and serves on the Advisory Committee for the Information Project for United Methodists.

✳ ✳ ✳ ✳ ✳

A companion perspective is offered by a parish pastor who was a contributor to @ Risk.

Irreconcilable Differences?

by Scott Campbell

At a recent family reunion we all agreed on a basic guideline. We would talk neither religion nor politics during the three days we were to be together. Since our family covers the gamut politically and encompasses similarly broad terrain religiously, it seemed like a prudent step. It more or less worked. The agreement did not prevent like-minded folk on one side of the divide from the occasional side huddle to bemoan the latest war-mongering atrocity by the Bush Administration, or those on the other from decrying the idiocracy of the Episcopalians in voting to install a gay bishop; but no one was at another's throat for the three days, and we all parted amicably, and still consider ourselves to be a part of the same family.

What works for three days, however, may not hold up over several centuries. The time has come in The United Methodist Church to talk about everything families finally need to talk about. Do we have enough in common with one another to keep our union intact, or are there differences so deep and so wide that the center can no longer hold?

In *United Methodism @ Risk* I argued that the decision of the General Conference of 1808 to restrict further changes to our doctrinal standards was a pivotal moment in the life of the church. To elaborate further, that decision impeded our ability as a church to grow gracefully together and to incorporate new understandings into our doctrinal formulations. It locked us into looking at the world through a set of nineteenth-century theological lenses. We did not forge a new consensus around significant doctrinal issues as we matured, nor did we adopt contemporary language to express our most fundamental beliefs. To this day we have no built-in mechanism for theological revitalization. As a result, we have found ourselves for the last thirty or more years trying to deal legislatively with what are decidedly theological questions. We have voted yes or no to a whole set of hastily conceived propositions rather than doing the long hard work of theological renewal that being the church demands. We now find ourselves a divided church, separated by widely divergent worldviews.

Further, our polity is based upon a number of assumptions that no longer hold. For instance, pastors have traditionally been assumed to be somewhat interchangeable.

While the system has always accounted for differing gifts and styles among pastors, they were considered to be doctrinally homogenous. Bishops, so the thinking goes, ought to be able to appoint any pastor to any church and know that the tradition would be well served. The third restrictive rule in the constitution reflects the conviction that central deployment of pastors is essential to the character of United Methodism. It forbids changes in the episcopacy or the itinerant general superintendency.

Here is the dilemma: Bishops are required to be guardians of the doctrinal standards of the church (that is, The Articles of Religion, The Confession of Faith, The General Rules, and the sermons and notes of Wesley) and to faithfully honor that responsibility in their appointment making. Yet, there are many pastors, including many bishops, who no longer find the traditional expressions of our doctrinal heritage adequate to meet the challenges of the day. They believe that doctrine must be continually reinvigorated as we understand more fully the revealed word of God. What is a bishop to do with a pastor who says, "I no longer believe in the bodily resurrection of Jesus Christ"? The solution for much of the twentieth century was akin to Bill Clinton's "don't ask, don't tell" policy around gays in the military. Bishops didn't force the issue. But now, in an increasingly polarized church, there are vocal advocacy groups like the Coalition for United Methodist Accountability (CUMA) whose entire mission is to hold contemporary leaders accountable to a certain reading of the doctrinal standards. They use the judicial processes of the church to enforce compliance. It is now the bishops whose hands are being forced.

Is it too late? Can anything be done to heal the wounds of the last century and forge a truly *united* Methodist Church in the next? Everything in me wants to shout, "It is not too late!" but I fear it may be. I love The United

Methodist Church, and the thought of it coming undone is more than painful to me. Yes, there are no simple solutions. Temporary agreements to smooth over our differences will not work. If there is any hope, it will require radical surgery to save the patient. Here are some options we ought to be considering:

- We should lift the first restrictive rule and then commission a broadly representative group of scholars, bishops, pastors, and laypersons to rewrite the Articles of Religion and the Confession of Faith to better reflect contemporary understandings. Efforts could be made to find common language that lessens our differences. Periodic revisions should be understood as an ongoing responsibility of the church.
- We must develop greater sensitivity to regional differences in the church, admitting that one size no longer fits all. We should delegate certain disciplinary responsibilities to the annual conferences rather than the General Conference. For example, conference boards of ordained ministry could have greater latitude in determining standards for admission to ministry.
- We might explore the creation of nongeographical jurisdictions based upon theological outlook. Conferences could opt to join the jurisdiction that best matched their theological perspective. Perhaps there could even be provision for local churches to participate.

If none of the above proves possible, perhaps it is time to think about moving toward some division. One would hope that division would not have to be divisive, but could be characterized by a partnering relationship between the two resulting bodies. Could a divided church still find ways to cooperate in mission to the world, even if they no longer were able to share the same doctrinal perspectives? I suspect they could and we might all be the stronger for directing our efforts toward ministry instead of against one another.

Scott Campbell is the pastor of the Harvard-Epworth United Methodist Church in Cambridge, Massachusetts. He teaches part-time at Harvard Divinity School, writes a regular column for Zion's Herald, and is the director of the Network for International Congregations. He wrote a chapter on doctrine and co-authored the study guide for United Methodism @ Risk.

* * * * *

Another plea for constructive conversations comes from another region of the country.

Words Will Kill You Dead

Advice from an Unauthorized and Self-appointed Referee of The United Methodist Church

by Rebekah Miles

When our four-year-old complained about being teased at preschool, her father taught her the old saying, "Sticks and stones may break my bones, but words will never harm me." The next day Anna reported that she had been teased again, so we asked how she had responded. "I told them, sticks and stones will break your bones, but words will kill you dead."

Once again, we are battling it out with the bloodiest weapon known to United Methodists—words. I am confident that we United Methodists spend more time wading in each other's blood than we do preaching the blood of Jesus. These fighting matches are as much a part of our tradition as potlucks and hymn-singing. I hope to see a lasting peace within our fellowship someday—perhaps when Jesus comes again. In the meantime, I would settle for a cleaner fight. If I were appointed the referee for United Methodist fights, I would offer some advice, beginning with Anna's insight.

We United Methodists have a way with words, and sometimes that way is deadly. We should not only watch our own language but also hold our more rash brothers and sisters accountable. The judicious have a responsibility to temper the injudicious. When Bishop Joseph Sprague refers to United Methodists who believe in classic claims like the Virgin Birth and physical resurrection as neo-literalists and idolatrous, somebody besides evangelicals, preferably liberal bishops, should go to him and say, "This is over the line." When Mark Tooley of the Institute for Religion and Democracy writes in his most cynical, cutting voice (which is most of the time), somebody besides the folk on the left—preferably members of the IRD board or its donors—should go to him and say, "This is not acceptable." If a few leaders and spokespeople of our organizations fail to show restraint, then it falls to the rest of the leadership and membership to restrain them.

Of course the intemperate words are not the only ones that kill. United Methodists on both the right and the left claim that the representatives of the other side have misrepresented the truth on occasion. This is one of the few cases where I agree with both groups at the same time. We need to be more careful not only about what we say, but also about what others say. We need to check up on each other's facts. When a spokesperson for an organization to which we belong tells only part of the truth, we need to investigate and then complain loudly. Perhaps the United Methodist News Service, the *United Methodist Reporter,* and other similar organizations could make it a regular practice to check out the claims made by United Methodist organizations on all sides.

We have a democratic process with clear rules set out

in our *Discipline.* It is a highly political system, and any-body can play. Some leaders have complained that the caucuses (left and right) have politicized the process. Let's be honest. The process was political all along, and a few powerful cliques used to provide most of the players. The main difference now is that we play the game more openly and have more groups joining in. The Black Methodists for Church Renewal did not make the process political, but simply insisted on their right to join the game. Critics of the conservative Good News and the Confessing Movements complain that they are a part of a well-organized, well-funded effort to change the church. Of course they are. The problem is not that the conservative renewal groups are too organized, but that the other groups who are com-plaining are not organized enough. This is the game. It is easy to complain about the game, the church, or some of the players, but the only way to change the game, the church, and its processes (including the rules by which the game is played) is to play the game and to play it well.

United Methodists across all lines should care about doctrinal tolerance for two reasons: pragmatic realism and the gospel. First, pragmatic realism. If one includes within our official doctrine Wesley's *Standard Sermons and Notes on the New Testament,* as most experts do, one should not be excessively strict about doctrinal purity. Any United Methodist who cannot find something to dis-agree with in all of those documents is not reading care-fully enough. Even Wesley changed his mind about some claims in his *Standard Sermons and Notes.* Of course, on the positive side, if we held every clergyperson and member accountable to every word of our doctrinal stan-dards and threw out anyone who disagreed, we would eliminate all the big problems of The United Methodist Church because there would not be any United Methodists left to cause any problems!

Our commitment to tolerance is grounded in something deeper. We value tolerance because we love and are a part of the body of Christ. If we really are one church, one body, then we must hear each other out—for the sake of the body and the truth. Methodists have long believed that Christians can learn from one another as they come together to interpret Scripture, bringing to this interpretation of Scripture an array of resources. (These days the list usually includes tradition, experience, and reason.) Any person could be wrong about some point of interpretation and could be helped in responsible Christian conferencing. This does not mean that the truth about God is changing, but that our understandings of the truth are always subject to error and correction. Open theological discussion is essential to good theology and good doctrine.

United Methodists across all lines should care about doctrine. Our doctrine is our church's teaching about who God is, how God works, and how humans can respond. What could be more important than that? If we disagree about doctrine, then let's get clear about our disagreements and about the official teachings of the church. Contrary to popular opinion, our official teachings can be changed. It would be very difficult, but technically possible, to change them. In the meantime, our doctrine as outlined in the *Discipline* is our official teaching. This is what full clergy members have promised to preach and maintain. We may all have a few quibbles with something in Wesley's sermons and notes, but if a particular clergyperson cannot preach and maintain some of the major claims of our doctrine, then that person faces a serious conflict of conscience. I am convinced that the church is better off if these cases remain matters of conscience rather than matters for church trial.

United Methodist politics is the closest thing many clergy have to a sporting event. As much as we hate to admit it, many of us love the game. And many of us become so caught up in the political game that we forget, in our worst moments, our ultimate goal—making disciples of Jesus Christ or, in Wesley's words, "reforming the nations and spreading scriptural holiness" across the land. If we forget our primary goal, then all of our words—however polite, however accurate, however tolerant, however doctrinally or politically correct—will come to nothing. Anna is right, words will kill you dead. But even the right words put to wrong ends will never bring life. Ultimately, only God's Word brings life. The least we can do is not let our words get in the way.

Rebekah Miles, Associate Professor of Ethics at Perkins School of Theology, Southern Methodist University, is a lifelong United Methodist and a clergy member of the Arkansas Conference where she was elected as a delegate to the 2004 General and Jurisdictional Conferences. She is one of many scholars produced by the Foundation for Theological Education. She is a co-author of Wesley and the Quadrilateral *and is the author of* The Pastor as Moral Guide *and* The Bonds of Freedom: Feminist Theology and Christian Realism, *as well as many articles in Wesley studies, Christian ethics, and practical theology.*

* * * * *

Our final essay comes from the long-tenured senior minister of a very large United Methodist Church who discusses an issue that is high on the agenda of a variety of large American institutions, including national political parties, the Southern Baptist Convention, the producers of consumer goods and services, the Evangelical Lutheran Church in America, institutions of higher education, the Episcopal Church USA, the "Big Four" national television networks, The United Methodist Church, the United States Senate, the Roman Catholic Church in America, and the large public high schools. This is the widening gap between the generations born before 1960 and those born after 1960, between producers and consumers, and between the donors of the dollars for charitable causes, and the institutions seeking to receive those charitable dollars.

The Disconnect Is Real, But Why?

by Norman Neaves

Daniel Church is the General Secretary of the General Council on Ministries of The United Methodist Church. Recently, when addressing a national convocation of United Methodist musicians, he began by noting that our United Methodist connection is in the process of disconnecting. The reason, he said, is because of "a creeping tide of congregationalism" that is showing up everywhere.[1]

We've heard the argument many times now in the last couple of decades. Churches are more interested in spending money on themselves than they are in spending money on others. Churches turn to other publishing houses than The United Methodist Publishing House for many, if not all, of their curriculum resources. Churches choose to sing songs that have been written by certain contemporary songwriters rather than stick strictly to the denominational hymnal. And hence we are facing, according to Mr. Church, "a creeping tide of congregationalism" that is threatening the very existence of the United Methodist connection.

But would we be willing to consider that the disconnect is every bit as much the responsibility of the denominational hierarchy as it is that of these congregations to which Mr. Church refers?

Instead of reining in these congregations that apparently no longer conform to someone's idea of United Methodist protocol, does the denomination itself need to be reined in for losing touch with hundreds upon thousands of United Methodists who no longer speak the same language? Could it be that our denominational disconnect is occurring not only and simply because of congregational disloyalty and self-centeredness, but also because of congregational disgust and dismay with certain faith directives and missional positions with which it simply cannot concur? Or even more painfully, might it be said that almost all of the big pronouncements and rulings of the Church at its highest levels generate interest among only a tiny fraction of The United Methodist family and really has little, if any, meaning for the vast majority of the rank-and-file people of our denomination?

The assumptions behind the questions basically are the same ones that motivated a previous General Conference to strongly consider moving one of the denomination's largest boards out of New York City and closer to the heartland of America. It was deemed that the board members needed to be located in an environment where a more representative United Methodist constituency lives, that the Church at its hierarchical level simply had grown out of touch with, and perhaps resistant to, the real ethos of United Methodism. But somehow the denomination managed to work around that request and eventually to justify remaining in New York City—which might well have been the correct decision to make in light of other factors that subsequently were considered. But instead of the gap between the top and the bottom closing to some extent, it would seem that it has widened even more precipitously, and now threatens the denomination's very existence even more.

I am amazed at the number of United Methodist people who no longer feel connected to the connection. I'm told that previous generations did, and maybe that explains why those who feel most connected today are largely adults in their sixties and seventies and up. But I know, as virtually every pastor who works at the congregational level knows, that today's adults who are in their twenties, thirties, forties, and fifties basically do not feel that connection at all. There are always exceptions, of course, but clearly they are exceptions to the rule and not the rule itself. And if that particular constituency does not feel connected to the connection—if, in fact, they feel connected to their local congregation and largely that's the extent of their connectedness—then somehow, one would have to conclude, the connection itself is in grave danger.

There are at least three alternatives to this unfortunate disconnect for the denomination to consider, at least as I see it. One is for the denomination to place the blame on these dissident congregations and to bemoan and decry their lack of loyalty and their proclivity toward so-called "consumerism" and "self-centeredness." But simply placing blame only exaggerates the alienation even further and finally isn't helpful. Nor is it helpful for these congregations to do the same thing in the direction of the denomination.

A second alternative is for the denomination to assume that the problem with these certain congregations lies in their not being properly educated about what United Methodism is all about. They need pastors who will teach them about United Methodist theology, history, and polity, and who will keep them informed on current issues facing the denomination. But personally, I'm afraid that's a misdiagnosis. The issue is much deeper than simply assuming that more education and enlightenment can turn around these congregations. There are those who are extremely well-informed and who are very displeased with the direction in which the denomination seems to be heading—and these are found on both ends of the conservative/liberal spectrum as well.

The third alternative is for the denomination to realize that it is losing touch with its grassroots constituency more and more (and not necessarily for the same reasons, either), and that unless attention is paid to that growing breech and a posture of responsiveness is developed at the highest levels of the Church, the time will come soon when there will not be enough followers to support the visions and the agendas of the so-called "leaders." Unresponsiveness leads to irrelevance; irrelevance leads to disinterest; disinterest breeds apathy; and apathy eventually produces a quiet and yet steady attrition like we've been seeing over the past thirty years. And how much further does it have to go before we realize that the whole structure could well collapse?

Wasn't it T. S. Eliot who said, "This is the way the world ends/Not with a bang but a whimper"?[2] And I'm sure many of us are now hearing the clear groanings of that whimper.

It's somewhat ironic to me that at the same time Wesley was doing his great work in England, small groups of dissenters were making plans to leave their homeland and to travel on small boats to another land across the sea where they could fulfill their dreams. They felt that the situation in England was hopeless, that the powers of that time had other agendas to fulfill and really didn't listen to them or take their concerns very seriously at all; and so they left quietly to establish themselves somewhere else.

But Wesley himself seemed to understand them and to be sympathetic with their concerns. And he worked with them to set up little Methodist societies in this strange new land, and appointed Coke and Asbury to work with them and to help them flourish; and certainly they flourished indeed. All the while, the powers in the palace and in parliament back home in London went on with their "business as usual" and missed an extraordinary opportunity that momentarily was on their doorstep.

I'd like to believe that the gap between the top and the bottom could be brought closer together in United Methodism. However, I do have real concerns that possibly it might never happen—and what a great shame that would be.

Norman Neaves is the senior minister of Church of the Servant in Oklahoma City, Oklahoma. In 1968 he was appointed to serve as the founding pastor of that congregation. Currently, it is among the two dozen largest United Methodist congregations in America. One explanation for the growth is the Church of the Servant has been able to attract, serve, and challenge an unusually large number of people born after 1950.

CHAPTER FIVE

WHAT IS
NON-NEGOTIABLE?

O ne approach to designing a new future for The United
Methodist Church could begin with the declaration,
"Everything is on the table! Nothing is non-negotiable.
We are free to design a new church for this new millennium with-
out any limitations."

Given the age and state of health of the people who will design
a ministry plan for the future of the UMC, it is highly unlikely
their assignment could be completed before at least 80 percent of
them have died, if every issue is open for negotiation. Therefore
consideration should be given to reducing the length of that
agenda. Californians proved they have the capability to choose a
governor from a ballot with one hundred thirty-five names, but it
is unlikely that more than 10 percent of the leaders designing this
new ministry plan will be from California.

What is non-negotiable? Here are four issues that this observer would place on that list.

Everyone Leaves!

If it becomes clear that the intradenominational quarreling in this branch of American Methodism is going to lead to schism, the consequence of many earlier quarrels within American Methodism as well as in contemporary American Protestantism, the decision should be made that this resolution will not be designed to produce "winners" who stay and "losers" who leave. Since a "win-win" resolution does not appear possible, that eventual resolution should be designed as a "lose-lose" plan. Every congregation loses. Every congregation will lose its current denominational identity. Every congregation will have to purchase new letterheads, redesign its website, and replace the words on the sign in front of the building. Every ordained minister will have to apply for a new denominational affiliation. Every layperson will have three choices: (1) to switch denominational affiliation, (2) switch congregational affiliation, or (3) to do both, switch to a different congregation affiliated with a different denomination.

Given the number and variety of the current intradenominational quarrels, no one should be able to declare, "My side won! They left, we stayed. Therefore the onus for our split is on them, not us." If it is too late to create a win-win scenario, every party should be a loser.

The Exit Fee

One resolution of the conflict produced by the Methodist-EUB merger in 1968 was a few dozen EUB congregations were permitted to leave and to retain title to their real estate. They could not, however, retain that denominational name. More recently other denominational mergers in American Protestantism have "opened the window" for congregations to depart and retain title to their property.

Any resolution of the current conflict within this branch of American Methodism probably will open the door for some congregations to leave. That is one side of this issue. The other side is that both the former Methodist and former EUB pension systems are based on the assumption that future generations should carry at least part, if not all, of the financial responsibility for liabilities incurred by earlier generations. In simple terms, every annual conference has a less than fully funded liability for the retirement benefits of United Methodist clergy. In addition, the number of retired clergy is expected to triple between 1965 and 2010, and the number of surviving widows of deceased ministers will at least quadruple. In 1965 the ratio of retired clergy to confirmed membership was 1 to 1,600. In 2001 that ratio was 1 to 550. It also should be noted that the annual cost of the benefits (pension plus health insurance) have been increasing at a far faster pace than the increase in congregational receipts. The amount of that unfunded liability varies, depending on the assumptions used in calculating it. The full list is too long to discuss here, but a few will illustrate the complexity of this issue.

1. What is the assumed life expectancy of a retired minister? In 2003, a new actuarial table projected the probable life expectancy of the average white sixty-year-old male to be four years longer than did the 1980 table. We also know males in white-collar occupations have a longer life expectancy than males in blue-collar jobs. Likewise, on the average, college graduates live longer than do Americans who never completed high school.

2. What is the projected age at retirement for United Methodist ministers?

3. What benefits will they receive between their retirement and age 62? Between retirement and age 65? Will the annual conference subsidize health insurance for all retired ministers? Or only those who retire at age 65 or later? Or only for those who retire before 2005? Or, will there be no subsidy for health insurance for retirees after age 65? Will the conference subsidize

health insurance for survivors after the death of that retired minister?

4. What will be the pension rate for each year of service before 1982?

5. What is the anticipated annual rate of return on the investments in the accounts that will fund those retirement benefits? Is it 5 percent per year? 7 percent? 9 percent? 4 percent?

6. Which of the current practices can be changed? Or, can benefits be reduced only for future retirees? Or only for the newly ordained?

One option is to leave the retirees holding a partially empty bag. Another is to place this financial liability only on congregations that elect to continue their affiliation with their present annual conference. This proposal declares that congregations choosing to sever their affiliation with this denomination cannot leave without paying their fair share of that unfunded liability.

One-half of a potential resolution is in the first of these two non-negotiable issues. The second is that every congregation pays the equivalent of an exit fee. This will require every annual conference to (1) calculate the amount of money required to fully fund all promised retirement benefits, and (2) distribute that unfunded liability among the current congregations, with a clearly stated date when the payment must be made. If payment is not made by that date, the conference can and will dissolve that congregation, sell the assets, and use the proceeds from that sale to help cover that unfunded liability.

If a congregation chooses to disaffiliate, it may do so by first paying this exit fee and thus retaining title to its property. If that option is rejected, the conference will dissolve that congregation, sell the assets, and use the proceeds to reduce that unfunded liability. One way or another, every congregation will contribute its fair share to eliminate this unfunded liability. The old precedent of deferring this to future generations will be broken.

One reason for making this a non-negotiable issue is fairness. The parishioners who benefit from the services of a pastor should pay both the current and future costs of that minister's current service.

A second reason is clarity. This will give every minister, both active and retired, a clear statement of promised future retirement benefits. Most pastors have an "understanding" of future retirement benefits. This will require each conference to provide a clearer promise of those future benefits. For example, for those receiving a pension for years served before 1982, will that rate for prior service be increased every year, or only if the funds are available? Will the early retiree receive at least a partial subsidy for the cost of health insurance? Will that subsidy cover only the pastor, or the pastor and dependents?

A third reason is equity. These promised benefits have been earned. They should be guaranteed. (Personal disclaimer: For the benefit of anyone who might suspect a conflict of interest, less than 1 percent of our retirement income comes from the pre-1982 defined benefit pension plan, and zero percentage of our health care costs are covered by a retirement plan of any annual conference or other religious organization.)

A fourth reason is the criteria to be used in evaluating alternative scenarios. Will a pastor examine each alternative on the basis of "How will this affect my retirement benefits?" or on the basis of "Which alternative will strengthen and undergird the mission and ministry of the congregation I am now serving?"

Finally, this should remove one potential basis for litigation opposing any change in the current organizational structure of this branch of American Methodism. That virus of litigation is alive and growing!

Trust the Living

Any new denomination created by a plan for the future will be designed on the assumption that future generations can be trusted. The constitution of any new denomination will not contain the restrictive rules found in the current United Methodist constitution. A majority of the living will be able to outvote a handful of the dead.

Names and Traditions

The laws governing the labels applied to products in the American marketplace do not apply to automobile manufacturers (we drive a Prism, but the shape does not resemble a prism) nor to religious bodies, but a new restrictive rule would control names. Any new denomination created by this process could not include the words "Methodist" or "Wesley" or "Wesleyan" unless the doctrinal statement or belief system was clearly Trinitarian and affirmed the divinity of Jesus and the resurrection of Christ. Likewise the name of any new denomination could not include the word "Evangelical" unless the doctrinal statement clearly affirms the authority of Scripture.

Finally, to reinforce the point that the resolution of the current quarreling will not produce both winners and losers but only losers, none of the new denominations or splinter groups that emerge will be allowed to use the name "The United Methodist Church." Everyone starts over, with a new name for a new future. That also means every First United Methodist Church will be required to choose a new name, as will Grace or Wesley or Centenary United Methodist Church.

This reinforces the conviction that every congregation, as well as every annual conference, must be required to choose between change A and change B. The illusion that the choice can be defined as between "status quo" and "change" will not be an option. A new church for a new millennium requires everyone to accept change.

What else do you believe should be added to this list?

CHAPTER SIX

MANY ROADS INTO THE FUTURE

The first five chapters have brought us to a fork in the road. Ahead of us are several attractive paths to the future. One is labeled "Denial." We won't take that road since just around the corner it terminates in a dead end.

Many readers will find the next fork more attractive. That signpost reads "Designing Ministries for the Twenty-first Century." We quickly discover why the plural of ministry is in that road sign. As we begin our journey down this road, we encounter a huge area designed for learning. Scattered throughout are scores of workshops, seminars, teaching churches, lecturers, and training events. Each one is marked by a huge sign indicating the theme of that learning opportunity. A number of our people immediately leave to participate in one labeled "Creating a New Future for Old First Church Downtown." A larger number elect to go to one hosted by the Ginghamsburg United Methodist Church south of Tipp City, Ohio, on the future of the open-country church founded before 1900. Another crowd gathers at the event hosted by The Church of the Resurrection in suburban Kansas City.

Most of our people, however, choose to stop at the one focusing on "How Your Conference Can Challenge Your Congregations." The first message we receive is that this workshop has been designed for leaders in high-commitment congregations and high-commitment annual conferences. A member from another group interrupts the leader by demanding, "Tell us what you mean by a high-commitment congregation." The response is, "We'll talk about that in a later session. A simple yardstick, however, is those congregations that project high expectations of anyone who wants to become a full member usually reports their average worship attendance exceeds their membership. A common ratio is the weekend worship attendance is 2 to 5 times the membership."

The next bit of advice we receive is to make resourcing of congregations to fulfill the Great Commission the top priority of our annual conference. We are warned that it will be somewhere between difficult and impossible to reverse years of numerical decline unless that becomes the top priority in the allocation of conference resources. We also are told that the bishop of our episcopal area, and all our district superintendents must actively affirm that priority. If that is impossible, we are advised to choose another workshop.

After an hour of other introductory comments and advice, the balance of the time is devoted to the six components of this high-commitment strategy. These are presented in the order of difficulty, with the easiest first and the most difficult last.

1. Encourage congregations averaging more than 450 at worship to become multisite churches. This calls for one congregation with one message, one name, one staff, one governing board, one budget, and one treasury and somewhere between 2 and 200 sites where people gather to worship God, to hear the gospel of Jesus Christ proclaimed, and to be challenged and equipped to be engaged in doing ministry. An increasingly common pattern calls

for the sermon to be delivered by way of videotape. That not only means the same message is proclaimed at every worship service at every site, but it also enables the pastor of that missionary church to deliver the same message five or five hundred times every weekend.

One version of this model calls for teams of two to five volunteers to staff each of dozens of small worshiping communities. One may be with single-parent mothers living in the same apartment complex. A second may be with residents of a mobile home park. A third may be with university students in their dorms. A fourth may be with a group of recent immigrants. An outstanding example of this version is the First Baptist Church of Arlington, Texas.[1]

Another version of this model is the self-identified large missionary church that, instead of planting what is intended to become an autonomous new mission, decides to share what it has learned about "How to do big church in the twenty-first century by becoming a multisite congregation."[2] Four of the essential resources in implementing this strategy are (a) a senior minister who is convinced God is calling this congregation to become a multisite church, (b) a cadre of volunteer leaders who share that vision, (c) a minister of missions who will help make it happen, and (d) one gifted campus pastor for each site who is content to preach on the third Sunday of August in even numbered years.

2. Encourage midsized congregations with the potential for growth to make the changes required for them to become large or very large churches.

3. Encourage congregations meeting in functionally obsolete physical facilities on an inadequate site, and/or at what has become a poor location, to make a fresh start by relocating to a larger site with better facilities.

4. Encourage congregations averaging fewer than 75 at worship to consider affiliating with or being adopted by a large multisite self-identified missionary church.[3] Those who feel threatened by this because they believe the future of American Protestantism is in the small church should be reassured that if as many as one-half of the 26,700 small UM congregations accept that challenge,

this denomination will still include approximately 13,000 small churches.

5. Plant new missions that are designed to become large congregations. The annual goal should be a number equal to 3 percent of the congregations in that annual conference. Thus the annual conference that includes 500 congregations would plant 15 new missions every year. The wealthy conferences may choose to send a solo pastor out to plant a new mission in the hope that 1 out of 5 will grow to an average worship attendance of 350 or more within five years, while the majority either will plateau as small churches or dissolve within a decade.

One thrifty approach is to circulate Requests for Proposals (RFP). This model identifies the sponsoring district and describes the primary constituency to be reached and served. Proposals are solicited from teams. Each team of three to seven persons describes their proposed design or model, how they will implement that design, the resources they will bring to this venture, and the resources they will require from the conference. A reasonable expectation is one-half of these proposals will be self-financing through pledges and contributions from individuals and congregations who are committed to the success of that proposal. The Conference Board of Missions reviews all proposals, selects the most promising, interviews the teams submitting these proposals, and recommends approval of the ones to be implemented.

6. Challenge those numerically declining and aging congregations to partner with the conference and cabinet in a customized renewal process. This is placed sixth because the inventory of pastors interested and able to lead this process is relatively small, and the demand is huge.

Our crowd goes off by itself to meet with one of the leaders of this learning opportunity to discuss how we can adapt this strategy to our various annual conferences. We are handed a thin booklet titled, "Suggestions for Implementing a Six-Point High-Commitment Growth Strategy for Annual Conferences." Among the suggestions are two we had heard earlier—make this the top priority for the conference and gain the support of the cabinet. The third suggestion surprised several in our crowd. "Take advantage of modern technology! That includes the private automobile, the telephone, teleconferences, videotapes, websites, recorded music, video projectors, excellent sound systems, and the computer. These resources make it easy for a missionary church to include a variety of sites within a hundred-mile radius of the central campus. These resources make it easy for the senior pastor, while on vacation in Italy, to deliver the sermon at every site."

The fourth point read, "It will be difficult to implement this strategy unless every appointment represents close to an ideal match between the gifts, skills, personality, experience, theological stance, and priorities of that minister, and the needs of that position."

The next point urged, "While fifteen- to twenty-year pastorates may be acceptable in some cases, the ideal goal will be for twenty years to be viewed as the minimum." This booklet went on to quote how the congregational ministers graduating from Yale College in the seventeenth and eighteenth centuries assumed that first call would be their only pastorate before death or retirement. Since death, not retirement, terminated the pastorates of many colonial ministers, the average tenure for each graduating class of ministers usually was only twenty to thirty years.[4]

The sixth suggestion was qualified with the statement, "Every congregation retains the right to ask the cabinet to select the pastor who will fill a vacancy." That paragraph, however, went on to declare, "It will be difficult to implement this six-point strategy without turning to a national ministerial market in selecting the pastoral leadership required to produce ideal matches and long pastorates."

The next suggestion shocked most of the people in our group. "We advise against adopting this six-point strategy unless your conference is prepared to engage a competent outsider to conduct an annual performance audit. Your conference hires an auditor every year to check the financial records. Your strategy to persuade people to accept Jesus Christ as Lord and Savior is far more important than accurate financial records. That annual performance audit is an essential component of this strategy. Without it, you will not be able to take the corrective actions required to achieve your goals. Without it, your conference will find it tempting to focus on inputs into your system, such as appointments, apportionments, clergy benefits, and meetings, rather than to measure the actual outcomes against the desired outcomes. You also need an outsider to conduct this performance audit. That eliminates the temptation insiders may have to conceal failure under a shield of diversionary rhetoric. This strategy cannot be implemented in an institutional culture that displays a high level of tolerance for mediocrity!"

The eighth suggestion was nearly as blunt. "You may decide to reverse the priorities for the top two components of this strategy if your conference includes only a few congregations averaging 450 or more at worship, *but* we urge you not to move the sixth component higher on your list. Revitalizing aging and numerically shrinking congregations is the most challenging and difficult assignment in this strategy. Start with the probable winners, not the probable losers!"

The response to the contents of this booklet was less than universal enthusiasm. One pastor declared, "I love this six-point strategy, but my conference will never invite an outsider to come in and evaluate what we're doing. NASA has done that twice, the Roman Catholic Church in America is doing that now, the Air Force Academy has done that, the Congressional Budget Office does that, and the American Red Cross has done that. In each case, one result is a lot of negative publicity. My conference is not looking for that."

Another added, "We would never go to a national market in appointments. Too many of our ministers depend on the appointment system for promotions."

A laywoman reflected, "It would be hard for my conference to make that switch from focusing on inputs into the system into concentrating on desired outcomes."

After a brief recess, our discussion continued, and finally our leader advised us that we should have made this the second or

third stop, not the first, on our tour of these learning opportunities. We are urged to go to the one with the sign that reads,
"Identifying Your Primary Constituency." As we head over there,
we stop for a short time to listen to a lecturer. One of the points
we still remember from that lecture was how the six predecessor
denominations placed a high priority on new church development. We were told that back in the 1880s, when the population
of the United States increased by only 13 million from 50 million
in 1880 to 63 million in 1890, the northern Methodists organized
4,000 new congregations, the southern church nearly 2,100, the
Methodist Protestant nearly 400 in that decade, the Church of
the United Brethren in Christ more than 500, the Evangelical
Association nearly 300, and the United Evangelical Church 73.
"That's a combined total of 7,356, or an average of 735 per year!"
declared this lecturer, "and that only counts those that were still
in existence in 1906! We don't know how many others were
started and didn't survive until 1906. For the past three decades,
in a country with a far larger number of unchurched people,
where the population increased by 25 million to 30 million rather
than 13 million, every decade, and in a denomination with far
more money, we haven't come close to averaging 75 new missions
a year!"

We continue to listen for a few more minutes as the lecturer
holds up a copy of the book *Organizing to Beat the Devil*, by
Charles W. Ferguson. Waving that book in the air, the lecturer
challenges us: "Two of the distinctive characteristics of American
Methodism are our passion for souls and our organizing skills.
Those were the two driving forces behind the planting of so many
new missions in the nineteenth century. Passion and the ability
to organize are the two essentials in any plan for ministry in the
twenty-first century."

Eventually we reach our destination. Here we are advised that
the first step in designing a ministry plan for the twenty-first
century is to identify our primary constituency. That advice
applies both to congregations and to annual conferences. Who is
our number-one constituency? Is the number-one priority in the
allocation of such resources as the pastor's time, the use of our

building, the schedule, the time and energy of volunteers, money, and our teaching ministries to take better care of our current members? Or, is the number-one priority to reach, attract, serve, challenge, and nurture the unchurched?

If you decide your primary constituency consists of people who do not have an active and continuing relationship with a Christian community, which slice of that population do you believe God is calling your congregation to reach and serve? We each were given a sheet of paper, printed on both sides, that described a variety of people who could be defined as unchurched. That long list included hard-core atheists; contented agnostics; agnostics on a self-identified search for meaning in life; believers who are ex-members of a congregation in which they were "burned out" (the maximum number of responsibilities for a volunteer is the number they are willing to accept plus two), or offended by the people in charge; newcomers to the community who are searching for a new church home; believers who are active members of a low-commitment congregation and are looking for a high-commitment church; disenchanted "cradle Catholics" searching for a Protestant church home; parents looking for a Sunday school for their young children; recent immigrants to the United States; teenagers who are theologically more conservative than their parents and have dropped out of their parents' church to join a parachurch movement; active church members who are disenchanted with their new pastor; newlyweds who came from two different religious traditions and are seeking a church that is acceptable to both; plus two dozen other categories.

We were advised that fewer than 10 percent of the congregations in The United Methodist Church can mobilize the resources required to implement a ministry plan that focuses on two or more of these unchurched populations.

"Begin by focusing on one group," we were urged. "As you move up the learning curve, select a second unchurched group and design a new ministry plan to reach that segment of the unchurched population."

As we wandered around looking for the next learning opportunity to investigate, one of our group members suddenly pointed out, "While most of our original group is still with us, these are nearly all volunteers and ministers who are largely concerned with congregational life. The folk who are heavily involved in and influential in denominational affairs have gone over there." As she spoke, she pointed to a signpost that read "For Those Who Enjoy Doing What Methodists Do Best."

Without further discussion, we all decided to go over there and try to discover what had attracted some of our colleagues. In this very large area beside the road were gathered three groups. Each one included scores of adults. Our folk decided to spend a little time on the fringe of each group and listen to what was being discussed.

Every participant in the first group we visited had a copy of a paperback book with a blue cover. The title was *United Methodism @ Risk: A Wake-up Call.* It quickly became apparent that the theme of this gathering was to oppose what was described as an exceptionally well-organized effort by a theologically conservative group to seize control of The United Methodist Church by electing the "right" people to be delegates to the General Conference. Much of the discussion focused on strategies to thwart this attempted takeover.

After listening to this discussion, our group quietly walked about two hundred yards to the east and listened in on the discussion going on among those participants. We were intrigued to see most of them also had a copy of that same blue covered paperback book *@ Risk.* The theme of this gathering appeared to be that the theologically liberal leaders had gained control of The United Methodist Church. The major complaint appeared to be that the core statements in the Articles of Religion in the constitution of The United Methodist Church were not simply being ignored. These doctrinal statements were being challenged as untrue, unreasonable, irrelevant, misleading, or the product of an obsolete approach to defining contemporary reality. One participant declared, "Heresy is not only being ignored, it is being approved as acceptable under the umbrella of freedom of the pulpit!"

We left that gathering to sit on benches on the fringes of the third group that had gathered in the space between the other two. Many of the active participants in this discussion referred to a copy of Ferguson's book *Organizing to Beat the Devil*. The theme of this discussion was an historical review of the skills of groups of Methodists to promote their cause. Among the examples cited were the organizing skills of those earlier Methodists and their decision to organize a new denomination in December 1784 rather than continue as members of the Church of England or join the Protestant Episcopal Church in America; the slow but gradual acceptance of married ministers; the design of camp meetings; the organizational skills of those schismatics who launched new movements and new denominations out of their Methodist constituency; the battle over slavery, and the organizational skills of those who opposed a compromise in favor of a split in the denomination; the organizing skills of the missionary Jason Lee in the settlement of Oregon; the campaign to impeach President Andrew Johnson; the split in the Church of the United Brethren in Christ over lodges; the early and successful efforts to thwart the reunion of the three Methodist denominations; the quarrels between the Germans and the English, between the east and the west and between the old and the new that led to a split in the Evangelical Association; and the Temperance Movement, a largely Methodist crusade, that led to the Eighteenth Amendment to the Constitution of the United States. This last victory marked the end of an era. A century earlier, Methodist circuit riders had been discouraged from marrying but allowed to peddle liquor. By the 1920s Methodist ministers were encouraged to marry but to abstain from the ownership, use, or sale of alcoholic beverages.

Another part of that discussion reviewed the successful efforts by the Methodists in the 1920s to defeat the campaign of a Roman Catholic to be elected president of the United States, and the failure of a similar effort in 1960.

As we left to resume our journey, we asked members of our group what they had learned. One reflected, "I now realize how difficult it will be back home to reach agreement on a strategy to reverse the melting of our ice cube, and on the priorities for the allocation of our resources in order to implement that strategy. Our annual conference is a collection of low-commitment congregations, and I doubt if we could win agreement to implement a high-commitment strategy. The combined average worship attendance for all our churches is less than one-half the combined membership."

Another observed, "I learned that for four decades after the Civil War, American Methodists used their organizing skills to plant tens of thousands of new missions. For the past three or four decades we have used our organizing skills for quarreling with one another."

"That's a good summary!" affirmed a third person. "In the post–Civil War era, with a few exceptions, we were organized around what we were for—the planting of new missions. For most of the twentieth century, however, we were organized around what we're against. We've been organized against demon rum, Roman Catholicism, how others interpret Scripture, the growth of individualism, the demand for self-determination, gambling, federal financial aid being sent directly to the public schools,[5] white racism, American foreign policy, parental choice for the education of children age six to seventeen, and a larger role for the laity. Do you think that in the twenty-first century we can find a cause we can all agree to support?"

"Most of the members of my annual conference identify with one of a half dozen caucuses or special interest groups," reflected a pastor. "We would need the support of at least three of them to adopt and implement the church-growth strategy we were introduced to earlier. I doubt if we could enlist that much support for so many changes."

As we prepared to depart from that collection of learning opportunities, we passed two others. The signpost at one read "The Road to Oblivion," and the other read "The Road to Irrelevance." As we walked by, one of our group commented, "I know several people who have the experience required to lead either one of those workshops."

Those reflections introduce the last chapter in this book. What are the other paths into the future for The United Methodist Church? Can the leaders of this denomination agree on which path to follow? Will these leaders decide to patch that old wineskin, or to replace it?

CHAPTER SEVEN

REPAIR OR REPLACE?

This book is intended to stimulate creative planning for the future of this branch of American Methodism for the twenty-first century. To be compatible with contemporary culture, that requires offering people choices.

Three choices were identified in the previous chapter. One is denial. Sooner or later that leads to a dead end. A second is to attempt to implement a strategy designed for high-commitment churches in a low-commitment religious body. A third is to continue to choose sides between the folk from Athens and those from Jerusalem on biblical interpretation.

This final chapter describes a dozen other scenarios. Several of them will be far more controversial than others, but The United Methodist Church currently includes several thousand members with years of experience in quarreling over alternative roads into the future.

All who have read this far know they are dealing with a list builder, so here is another short list.

I. Empower the Laity to Decide

The scenario least likely to be given serious consideration affirms the right of self-determination and gives the laity a more influential voice. In a designated month, perhaps May or October or January, every congregation would be asked to set aside a two-hour session every week for four weeks. Those eight hours would be devoted to a serious study of the Articles of Religion. Early in the following month every confirmed member would receive a paper ballot offering that member two choices:

> Do you favor retaining the Articles of Religion exactly as found in the Constitution of The United Methodist Church? Or, do you favor the creation of a national study committee that would be asked to prepare two revisions of the Articles of Religion, one a traditional statement and one significantly more liberal? (That wording probably should use more neutral language.)

> ____Retain   _____Study Committee

If the study committee option received the majority of the votes, that would require a more complicated process to delete the restrictive rules from the present constitution.

A year later a similar referendum could be held to ask members to choose between retaining the present system of governance and accountability or revising it.

One obvious objection to this scenario is it gives equal weight to the vote of that marginal member who attends church once or twice a year, and to the preference of the most active, deeply committed, and thoughtful members. That is acceptable in a participatory democracy but not in a representative system of governance.

II. Delete the Restrictive Rules

Another scenario unlikely to win broad support is based on the assumption that the living, not the long dead, should write the rulebook that governs a voluntary association. One objection to that is The United Methodist Church is not a voluntary association, it is a covenant community. That is partially true, but the heart of our covenant is real estate, the appointment system, and apportionments, not the allegiance of individuals. In those Christian congregations that identify themselves as covenant communities, the departure of any member must be approved by either the governing board or a congregational vote. That is *not* a common practice in this denomination!

This scenario probably could be implemented by calling a special three-day session of the General Conference. The first day would be devoted to study and answering questions on the issue to be voted on during the second day. The packet of information on this issue would have been sent to each delegate eight months earlier and made widely available.

The morning of the second day the delegates would vote on a proposal to dissolve The United Methodist Church. If that proposal received a majority of 60 percent or more, the afternoon would be devoted to a vote on the proposal to create a new denomination that would be a carbon copy of the current structure except for deletion of the restrictive rules from the constitution.

If that proposal failed, the third day would be devoted to approval of plan B.

III. Is White Racism the Problem?

Those who are convinced white racism is a cancer on the body and soul of this branch of American Methodism could advocate a relatively simple and quick course of action. A special called session of the General Conference could meet in late April 2006 (when Easter falls on April 16). That three-day session could vote on the first day to dissolve The United Methodist Church, effective December 31, 2006. Every congregation would be offered three options.

1. Refuse to pay the exit fee, and the congregation will be dissolved.

2. Pay the exit fee and petition for membership in one of the three large black denominations in American Methodism. If their petition is rejected, they could (a) dissolve, (b) petition another one of those three denominations for membership, or (c) design their own future.

3. Pay the exit fee and choose their own future. Several hundred would choose to be independent or nondenominational congregations. Others would look for allies to create a new denomination. A couple of these could be for Korean American Methodists. Another could be a denomination for downtown Methodist congregations. A large number of congregations might choose to petition for membership in one of the remaining Protestant denominations.

This scenario also would call for the liquidation of all assets held by the various annual conferences and the national agencies (except for the United Methodist Foundation, the Board of Pensions, The United Methodist Publishing House, and the Commission on Archives and History). The expenditure of any of these funds from this liquidation process would have to be approved by the General Council on Finance and Administration.

Congregations planning to join one of these three black denominations could do so at any time between July 1, 2006, and December 31, 2008. This would give them time to raise the money required to pay their exit fee. It also would give the policymakers in the three black denominations time to define the criteria they would use to accept or reject applications.

All funds received from that liquidation of assets would be turned over to The United Methodist Foundation. Those with donor restrictions on their use would be administered by the foundation. The remainder would pay the "entrance fee" for join-ing one of the black denominations. This would be based on the combined membership of all congregations that affiliated with that denomination as of December 31, 2009. Members of con-gregations that did not choose to join one of the black denomi-nations, or were members of a church that dissolved, would have at least a year to join a congregation that did choose to build its future with a black Methodist denomination. Likewise, members of a congregation choosing to affiliate with a black denomination would have a year or so to decide "Is this the denomination for me?" in order to affirm their right of self-determination.

If, for example, on December 31, 2009, exactly 4 million United Methodist members had joined one black denomination and 2 million had joined each of the other two, The United Methodist Foundation in 2010 would transfer title to one-half of those assets to that first denomination and divide the remaining one-half equally between the other two.

We will visit a different version of a similar scenario at the end of this chapter.

IV. Don't Ask, Don't Tell

When confronted with that highly divisive issue of homosex-uality, the armed forces of the United States created the policy of "Don't Ask, Don't Tell." That also was the operational policy in this branch of American Methodism until recently. For most of their history the predecessor denominations included homosex-ual clergy, but the distinction between one's private life and the public realm kept this from becoming a divisive public problem.[1]

The current organizational structure of this branch of American Methodism asks scores of what could be considered to be intrusive "choose sides" questions. One set of these intrusive questions is asked by the conference board of ordained ministry of each candidate for ordination. Others are asked in the ordina-tion ceremony and when a minister requests membership in the annual conference. Other sets of intrusive questions are asked of parents who request baptism of their baby, of persons who seek to join a congregation, in the rituals for Holy Communion and marriage, and in the installation ceremonies for officers in the church.

One alternative could be to eliminate all these intrusive questions from the resources used in The United Methodist Church. A simpler alternative would be to add "It all depends" as one of the acceptable responses. For those who are looking for a Christian community that proclaims a precisely defined doctrinal position, the exit door will continue to be open and they will be free to find a new church.

Several readers will be quick to point out the big issue is whether the Judicial Council would approve this scenario. Others will insist this is the current operational policy in regard to theological beliefs, issues of human sexuality, the payment of apportionments, and denominational loyalty.

V. Buy a Bigger Umbrella

Unlike the Episcopal Church USA, most United Methodist ministers identify themselves as Protestant Christians. Relatively few Anglican priests identify themselves as Protestants. Despite that difference in the perspective of the clergy, both religious traditions, like the Roman Catholic Church, are organized on a foundation of distrust of local leadership. In many countries the Anglicans are organized with the province as the primary umbrella organization for dioceses. In the United States, however, the Anglicans are organized as one national church called the Episcopal Church USA, with nine geographically defined provinces. One possible resolution of the current internal conflict among Episcopalians in the United States is to delegate more authority to each province. That could be the place in the system, for example, that confirms the diocesan elections of bishops.

A parallel for United Methodists could be to expand the number of jurisdictions from five to twelve or fifteen. Five would be defined in geographical terms for geographically defined annual conferences that prefer the traditional system. The remaining jurisdictions could be a resource center for affinity conferences. For example, one jurisdiction could include several affinity conferences, each composed of congregations that are not served by a full-time resident elder. That jurisdiction might include 10,000 to 20,000 congregations, depending on how many choose a geographically defined conference.

Another jurisdiction might consist of four or five affinity conferences, one for large downtown churches, one for large two-site churches, one for large multisite congregations, and one for single-site megachurches. This jurisdiction might include only 5 percent of all UM churches, but account for one-fifth of all UM worshipers on the typical weekend. A third jurisdiction could include those affinity conferences that want to retain the Articles of Religion as their doctrinal statement. A fourth affinity jurisdiction could include those conferences that believe each congregation should be free to articulate its own doctrinal statement. This would parallel the polity of the United Church of Christ, in which every congregation has that constitutional right. The United Methodist Church would operate as one huge umbrella with an annuity board, the United Methodist Foundation, a publishing house, a commission on archives and history, and five other full-time staff members. Under that huge umbrella would be twelve to fifteen largely autonomous jurisdictions. Each jurisdiction would serve as the final court of appeal for individuals, congregations, and annual conferences engaged in a dispute. Each jurisdiction would be completely free to design the appropriate organizational structure for resourcing its conferences and congregations. A reasonable guess is no two would be alike.

Since this would open the door to congregations changing their annual conference affiliation, that exit fee described in the previous chapter would be charged every congregation, regardless of their choice of conference. That is the price tag on being able to choose your doctrinal position and your peers. Self-determination is a commendable goal, but it is *not* free!

VI. Endorse Diversity and Pluralism!

What could be the most popular scenario in this chapter is symbolized by the slogan "Open Minds, Open Hearts, Open Doors." The General Conference could approve a statement resembling this one: "We believe God is calling The United Methodist Church in the United States to be a Christian community that is demographically diverse and theologically pluralistic. We stand ready to welcome everyone." (That could be amended by stealing a slogan invented by someone else: "We welcome anyone who will welcome everyone.")

This scenario raises at least five questions, each more challenging than the previous one.

1. Could that statement win the support of the majority of the delegates to General Conference?

2. Is that scenario the most effective way to reach the generations of residents of the United States born after 1960? My travels and most of the research I have read strongly suggests these generations can be found in disproportionately large numbers in those congregations in American Protestantism in which the teaching and preaching is characterized by certainty rather than ambiguity or a pluralistic theology.

3. A much more challenging question arises when the focus is shifted to implementation. One strategy could call for creating a heterogeneous denomination consisting of nongeographical and homogeneous affinity annual conferences, each one composed of relatively homogeneous congregations. One conference could consist of congregations in which most of the members were born in Korea or married to someone who was born in Korea. Another of congregations in which most of the members were comfortable with a liberal interpretation of Scripture. A third of congregations in which most of the members were born in America but of African ancestry. A fourth of congregations in which most of the

members preferred to worship God in Spanish rather than English. This strategy was utilized by the Methodist Episcopal Church up through the early 1920s.

A second strategy calls for creating a heterogeneous denomination composed of heterogeneous conferences, but with an affirmation of "the homogeneous unit principle"[2] for congregations. Should the resident bishop of that episcopal area, including that annual conference, be a minister who believes in the divinity of Jesus, or one who is not a Trinitarian?

A third strategy would call for a heterogeneous denomination consisting of heterogeneous annual conferences with each conference consisting of heterogeneous and inclusive congregations. Is that on the list of realistic possibilities? Is it realistic to expect that each of the 18,000 United Methodist congregations now averaging fewer than 60 at worship could offer weekly worship services in Spanish, Mandarin, English, Korean, Polish, and one hundred other languages and dialects? Is it realistic to expect every UM congregation will offer an Easter service that celebrates the resurrection of Jesus Christ and also offer one in which the Resurrection is described as a myth?

4. The hill we have to climb to implement this scenario gets steeper when the time comes to design a polity for a heterogeneous denomination. One response is described by the $20-term "consociational theory." This resembles what United Methodists call "conferencing," plus the goal of a grand coalition that includes everyone (thus eliminating opposition), plus the power to act, plus an emphasis on guaranteeing minority rights. One consequence is many groups prefer to secede rather than join a grand coalition. Horowitz adds that the concept of consociational governance cannot work when there are deep internal divisions.[3] (That explains why chapter 3 is included in this book.)

5. The highest barrier to implementing this scenario appears near the top of this hill. How can a strategy for creating a heterogeneous American Protestant religious body that is organized to welcome anyone who will welcome everyone be implemented in a denomination in which the constitution demands doctrinal

homogeneity, in which the polity is a centralized command and control structure, and the core components of both the doctrinal statement and the polity cannot be changed?

One response could be to dissolve the present denomination and replace it by organizing a new denomination structured to support heterogeneity. A second response is to look at another scenario.

VII. Change the Light from Red to Green

One bright gleam of light in this dark tunnel is expressed by those who contend, "None of these issues are worth quarreling over in today's culture that affirms self-determination. Why not encourage each congregation to focus on ministry and put aside all these fringe issues. All that is required is to change from a permission-withholding system to a permission-granting system based on the assumption that United Methodist Christians can be trusted."

The good news is that transformation has been underway for many years. All that is required is for the General Conference to amend the *Book of Discipline* to legitimatize what have become widespread practices. This would require creating a new single-function national agency that could receive and approve waivers. Each request for a waiver from a congregation, an annual conference, or an ordained minister would be accompanied by a statement citing a contemporary practice that matches the request.

A dozen examples can be used to illustrate this procedure. If an elder wished to submit a unilateral request to fill a position about to be vacated by another elder, that minister could request a waiver to ignore the traditional appointment process. This is being done to fill vacancies on the faculties of UM seminaries, national denominational agencies, and pastoral appointments. If a congregation decided that rather than pay the cabinet to find a pastor to fill a vacancy, that congregation could request a waiver allowing it to conduct its own search for a pastor. If a congregation concluded the apportionment for the World Service Fund and other apportionments was too large, it could request a waiver allowing it to pay only 10 or 15 or 20 percent of the total apportionment. If a congregation decided to purchase resources from non-UM vendors rather than from UM agencies, it could request a waiver permitting that to be done. If an elder, after serious and prayerful deliberations, concluded, "In good conscience, I cannot agree with nor support one or more doctrinal statements in the Articles of Religion in the UM Constitution," that minister could request a waiver granting permission for that minister not only to publicly disagree with the Articles of Religion, but also to proclaim a completely different statement of religious beliefs. If a congregation decided to withdraw from this denomination and keep title to its property, it could pay an exit fee, request a waiver, and depart. If a layperson, an ordained minister, or an annual conference decided it did not want to abide by a decision by the Judicial Council, it could request a waiver. If a jurisdiction did not want to reduce the number of episcopal areas, it could request a waiver. If a congregation was dissatisfied with its pastor, a 70 percent vote by the members could generate a request for a waiver permitting that congregation to dismiss that minister. If a congregation decided it did not want to have a unit of the United Methodist Men or the United Methodist Women in its organizational structure, it could request a waiver. If a congregation decided to become a multisite church, it could request a waiver allowing it to override disapproval by the district superintendent. If a congregation decided to hire a minister from another denomination rather than a United Methodist pastor, it could request a waiver. If an Anglo congregation decided to organize a new worshiping community to meet in its building and be staffed by an immigrant pastor from Korea, China, India, Mexico, or Cuba, it could request a waiver to do so.

The key foundation stone for this reform is trust. The second is the right of self-determination. The third is precedent, and the fourth is equal treatment under the law. Laypersons and the clergy now have the right of unilateral withdrawal. Thousands exercise that right every month. Therefore why should not that right be extended to congregations?

The staff of this new agency will be required to grant each request for a waiver no later than five days after that request has been posted on the agency's website. The presumption is each request is valid. Therefore any person or agency or official opposing the granting of a waiver would have five days to file a protest alleging no precedents exist for granting that waiver. The presumption of legitimacy rests on the party requesting the waiver. The burden of proof that the precedent accompanying that request is not relevant rests on the party objecting to the granting of that waiver.

Within months the big fringe benefit of this reform will be the cross-fertilization of creativity. All across the denomination, United Methodists will be monitoring that website. Every once in a while (eventually a hundred times a day), a congregational or conference leader will respond to a specific request for a waiver, "Hey! If they can do that, we can too! Let's contact them to see what we can learn from their experiences."

Mixing trust, precedents, new experiments, and equal treatment could be one way to replace the bitterness generated by intradenominational quarreling with the job of creating the new. In that centuries-old debate between law and grace, it could move grace ahead of law.

VIII. A Free Market in Ministerial Placement

What may be the most radical scenario in this chapter places the blame for the melting of that big UM ice cube on the appointment system. The General Conference would rule that all current pastoral appointments would be terminated on June 30 of the next calendar year. Congregations could choose either to retain the services of their current ordained or licensed minister or ministers or to terminate that relationship. This moratorium on the traditional appointment system would include creating a system enabling each minister currently serving as a parish pastor, or seeking that role, to participate in a nationwide ministerial placement process. This would require creation of a new website and might require as much as $300,000 to design and operate it for fourteen months. One of the twin goals would be for congregational leaders to rejoice "We have a minister who matches what we need." The other goal would be every pastor could declare "This is where I believe God wants me to serve, and this is where I chose to serve." Ministers who had been serving in the parish ministry but did not receive an invitation would receive a termination payment equal to $3,000 for every five years they had served as a parish pastor.

Those termination payments could be paid as the first claim on the Ministerial Education Fund. Why? If the educational system failed to equip them to serve as parish pastors in the twenty-first century, that system should be liable for the warranty payment. Opening this door also would enable any of those 25,000 UM congregations unable to attract, challenge, pay, and retain a full-time and fully credentialed resident pastor to use this opportunity to choose the system they prefer for ministerial leadership in the future. This could be a circuit. It could be sharing a minister with a congregation of a different denominational affiliation. These congregations also could look at such options as partnering with a large UM congregation for leadership or petitioning to be adopted as one of several campuses for that large multisite UM church.[4]

IX. Leaders Should Lead!

At least a few readers will suggest that one of the scenarios for this chapter should begin with paragraph 527(3) of the *Book of Discipline*. This charges the Council of Bishops with the responsibility for "the oversight of the spiritual and temporal affairs of the whole church."

What does that mean? Does that mean the Council of Bishops has a responsibility to resolve the crisis described in @ *Risk*? Does that mean the Council of Bishops should attempt to reduce the quantity and emotional level of the contemporary intradenominational quarreling? Does that mean the Council of Bishops should accept the responsibility for the melting of the United Methodist ice cube? Who decides what "oversight" covers?

The rest of that sentence reads, "to be executed in regularized consultation and cooperation with other councils and service agencies of the Church." That raises the separation of powers issue. Who has the authority to define oversight? Who has the authority to initiate? Who has the authority to define the outcomes this huge system is expected to produce? Who decides where "the buck stops" when those desired outcomes are not produced?

Who defines what is an acceptable outcome? For example, as mentioned earlier, between 1960 and 2000 the population of California increased by 116 percent, but the reported membership of this denomination dropped from 324,367 for the two predecessor denominations in 1960 to 180,858 in 2000. Does that decrease of 42 percent represent an acceptable outcome? Does that come under that umbrella of "the spiritual and temporal affairs"? In Illinois those four decades brought an increase of 23 percent in population and a decrease of 45 percent in membership. In Ohio those two indicators were a plus 17 percent and a minus 33 percent. In Virginia a plus 78 percent and a minus 10 percent measured the pace of the retreat. In Texas the population increased by 118 percent, and the UM membership grew by 5 percent. In Michigan the population grew by 27 percent, while UM membership shrunk by 41 percent. Georgia experienced a 108 percent increase in population and a 19 percent increase in UM membership.

Those examples carry the discussion back to an issue identified in chapter 3, the growing disengagement between congregational leaders and the denominational system. Congregational leaders ask questions such as these: "Why is our conference reporting a decrease in membership when the population is increasing?" "Why are so many of our churches reporting a decrease in attendance while the megachurches around here are growing?" "We're held accountable, and sometimes even held up for ridicule, if we don't pay our apportionments in full. Who is being held accountable for the withering away of our denomination in this state?"

"Who is being held accountable for our retreat from the central cities and the older suburbs? Who is being held accountable for that increase in the number of very small congregations and for that decrease in the number averaging 35 or more at worship?"

One response is, except for payment of apportionments, The United Methodist Church trusts every member, every pastor, and every official to do their best. Therefore they are accountable only to God, not to any manmade institution.

Another response is the system is organized around entitlements, not accountability. Bishops are entitled to set their own priorities. Retired clergy are entitled to retirement benefits in addition to Social Security and Medicare. Each national agency is entitled to its traditional share of the apportionments. Annual conferences are entitled to a fair share of each congregation's income. Disenchanted members are entitled to switch their allegiance to a congregation in some other religious tradition that is organized around accountability.

A third response is the Council of Bishops was created to hold each bishop accountable to peers for what happens in that bishop's episcopal area.

A fourth response is, we have not decided whether bishops should fill the role of preacher or of leader. If they are preachers, freedom of the pulpit, academic freedom, the American right to free speech, and guaranteed tenure means they are accountable only to God for what they say. If, however, their role is defined as the leader of that episcopal area, only the bishops who serve one annual conference can be held accountable for what happens or does not happen in that conference. If a bishop's episcopal area includes two or more annual conferences, it would be unfair and unreasonable to hold that bishop accountable for everything that does or does not happen in each conference.

A rude response may be the best. If the Roman Catholic Church in America was able to function for decades without holding their bishops accountable for the actions of priests engaged in acts of pedophilia, what makes you believe The United Methodist Church can or should hold its bishops accountable for relatively minor concerns such as a shrinkage in membership or a retreat from the cities?

The current operational response appears to this traveler to be either (1) a system of accountability requires outsiders to meddle in someone else's business and we don't approve of that, or (2) there is no evidence to prove that the absence of accountability is the cause of this disengagement or disenchantment among congregational leaders.

The pragmatic response is accountability is an unattainable dream without at least an annual audit of performance measured against specific, attainable, and measurable goals. Modern technology, of course, has made it relatively easy to complete a monthly or weekly performance audit rather than the traditional annual audit.

Does the inclusion of the word *temporal* mean that the Council of Bishops should speak for the whole Church on issues of public policy such as taxation; a balanced budget; parental choice in choosing a tax-funded elementary or secondary school; American foreign policy; abortion; immigration; affirmative action; homosexuality; the environment; marriage; divorce; the punishment of criminals; and the minimum wage? If yes, does that mean the General Board of Church and Society should be abolished as redundant? Would an annual conference be free to adopt a resolution on a matter of public policy contrary to the policy articulated by the Council of Bishops? Would a congregation be free to advocate a policy contrary to that advocated by the Council of Bishops?

Does "oversight of the spiritual affairs" require the Council of Bishops to resolve the issue of biblical interpretation described in the book *United Methodism @ Risk?* Would this require a unanimous opinion by the members of the Council of Bishops? Or, could a majority support one interpretation while a minority would be free to advocate a completely different view? Or, would the majority rule, and the dissenters have the choice between silence and resignation on the most divisive issues?

These and other questions surface several issues that could eliminate this scenario from the list of potential responses to what is now a dysfunctional system. First, do the members of the Council of Bishops have the time to fulfill this oversight role? Second, do they possess the experience, expertise, and credibility required for this role? (The events of the past five years in American Christianity have not reinforced the credibility of any-one carrying the title "Bishop.") Third, does the present system of electing bishops at jurisdictional conferences mean it will be difficult to secure the desired level of unanimity on many highly divisive issues?

Fourth, as Pierre Manet, a French political scientist, has pointed out, two other dynamics in a system influence the con-sequences of a system based on the separation of powers. The first is, it is unlikely to be trouble-free if it is introduced into a system that has depended heavily on a command-and-obedience form of governance. Iraq is a contemporary example. Manet contends that the separation of powers is most likely to work in a system that has been built on a web of relationships designed to satisfy the individual best interests of each party. The other is the greater the influence of partisan interest groups, the more likely the separation of powers will produce what Stendahl described as "powerless hatred."[5]

One example of powerless hatred was the impeachment of President William Jefferson Clinton, which was not confirmed by the United States Senate. A second has been the recent series of attacks on President George W. Bush by Democratic senators.[6] A third was the success of the recent effort to recall the governor of California.

Finally, in an American culture permeated with distrust of cen-tralized authority, and experiencing a rising tide in support of the right of self-determination, is it realistic to expect the delegates to the General Conference will be able to agree to expand the operational authority of the Council of Bishops?

A more optimistic response to that question has been developed by a pair of respected United Methodist scholars, both of whom are experts in the history and polity of this branch of American Methodism. Russell E. Richey and Thomas Edward Frank con-tend the potential value of the "general superintendency" has yet to be fully realized. One change calls for election of bishops by the General Conference rather than by the five jurisdictional conferences. Another calls for creation of a full-time position for the person elected to serve as president of the Council of Bishops. A third calls for providing that office the necessary staff to support expanded oversight functions, including a mandate to research, propose, and advocate new directions in the mission of The United Methodist Church.[7]

X. Change the Subject

This observer's preferred scenario can be introduced with three short sentences. First, play the cards you've been dealt. Second, relax! Third, change the subject.

Every United Methodist member, either lay or clergy, born after 1808 has known (1) the doctrinal stance of the denomination they joined and (2) that the core components of the denomination on both doctrine and polity cannot be changed.[8] If a congregation or an individual is convinced it no longer is possible to live with that doctrinal statement with integrity or with that polity, the exit door is open seven days every week. Rather than fight for an unattainable goal, relax. Concentrate on making the present system work. In more specific terms, change the focus of the discussions from inputs into the system (doctrine, polity, rules, money, traditions, power, control, placement of ministers, apportionments, schedules, wealth, and so forth) to a greater emphasis on outcomes.

During the past two centuries members of this branch of American Methodism have quarreled over hundreds of issues. The short list includes these divisive issues: must a preacher be celibate to itinerate; the role of theological seminaries; dancing; card playing; music; whether a bishop can be a slave owner; secession; reconstruction in the South after 1865; membership in lodges and secret societies; opposition to or support for the Sunday school movement; the Virgin Birth; observance of the Sabbath; prohibition; indoor plumbing; the candidacy of a

Roman Catholic for the presidency of the United States; American foreign policy; civil rights; the role of women in the church; the divinity of Jesus; the authority of bishops; clergy benefits; federal aid to public schools; the resurrection of Christ; translations of the Bible; the power of the laity; mergers with other denominations; the title to church property; interdenominational cooperation; electricity in houses of worship; new church development; the location of national denominational agencies; and homosexuality.

Most of these and other divisive issues fall into one of eight categories: doctrine, polity, power and control, human sexuality, ecumenism, the impact of technology, competition, and public policy. A second common, but less than universal, characteristic is, most can be described as inputs into the system.

A quick review of the history of Christian faith on this planet, for example, reveals that followers of Christ have been quarreling over human sexuality from the fifteenth chapter of Acts through at least the spring of 2004.

Inputs into any system in the American culture tend to be divisive. Examples include leadership styles; values; ministerial appointments; the financial support of educational institutions; governance; schedules; the allocation of scarce dollars; boundaries; financial subsidies; and electoral campaigns.

The most effective strategy for transforming a collection of individuals and partisan groups into a unified group is to identify a common enemy and rally the people together against that common enemy.[9] A slogan or symbol such as "taxation without representation," slavery, the pope, Pearl Harbor, "foreign invaders," or the war on terrorism are examples. In other words, it is easier to unify people around the theme of "what we oppose" than it is to rally people around "what we are for." One example of that is candidates affiliated with the party out of office tend to articulate their opposition to the party and officials in office when campaigning for election.

This raises a problem for Christians who have been taught to "love your enemy." While exceptions do exist, the most effective organizing principles for Christians have been to rally people around missions and evangelism. Both of these can be described as outcomes of the system.

Could The United Methodist Church be reinvented so that evangelism and missions would join the care of today's members as the three central purposes of both congregations and denominations? Can the current pattern of identifying "enemies" and rallying people against a common foe as a tactic in intradenominational quarreling be replaced by a new pattern of organizing in support of ministry, missions, and evangelism? The answer to that question is "Probably not, unless the denominational culture is transformed."[10]

XI. Change the Culture

Back in 1906 the six predecessor denominations reported a combined total of 57,087 congregations in the United States. That averaged out to 1 congregation for every 1,475 residents of the United States. At the end of 2003 The United Methodist Church included approximately 35,000 congregations in the United States, a ratio of 1 congregation for every 8,275 residents. What will that ratio be in year 2025? In 2050?

If we add to that number of 57,087 congregations that existed at the end of 1906 the number of new missions launched in 1907 through 2003, that total comes to at least 75,000 and probably exceeds 80,000. Deduct 35,000 from 75,000; the result is more than one-half of the congregations that existed in 1906 or were planted since 1906 no longer exist! What happened?

Another significant question is what will be the ratio of constituents to population? Is this denomination retreating from the ecclesiastical scene all across America, or primarily in the North and West?

This observer is convinced that answer is not preordained. This pilgrim believes God gave human beings an amazing degree of freedom to shape the future. Nowhere on this planet is that more obvious than in the United States. A persuasive argument can be made that the best years in the history of this branch of

American Methodism lie in the future. This optimist is convinced that if three questions can be answered in the affirmative, the future of this denomination can be better than the past. Unfortunately, however, these could turn out to be highly divisive issues.

The first question focuses on the culture of this denomination. Rewriting the rulebook will be of little value unless the culture is transformed. Patching old wineskins will not help unless the culture is changed. That parallels the top issue on the agenda of the Air Force Academy; United Airlines; the Enron Corporation; the government of California; Alabama; NASA; scores of large foundations that spend too much on "administration" and allocate too little for charitable causes; many large universities; the Roman Catholic Church in America; the United States Senate; most huge public high schools; and *The New York Times*.

Over the past two centuries the culture of this branch of American Methodism has reinforced the distrust of congregational leaders, refused demands for greater accountability to the constituencies, and tolerated mediocrity in a society that expects excellence. One consequence is the organizational structure continues to be built on vertical relationships when the success stories are found in horizontal partnerships. Another consequence is this denomination continues to function as a regulatory body when the demand by congregations is for resources.

That introduces a demographic issue. A reasonable estimate is the number of adults in America who believe they are called to regulate the beliefs and behavior of others has doubled since 1950. Concurrently, however, the number of Americans who feel a deep need for someone to regulate their beliefs and behavior has plummeted.

A second relevant change can be seen on the American ecclesiastical landscape. How do you justify the existence of a denominational system? Among the historic reasons denominations were expected to examine and recommend candidates for ordination; to ordain or license adults for a full-time Christian vocation; to enlist, equip, support, and supervise missionaries; to plant new missions; to publish hymnals and other books; to search out and combat heretical teachings; to create, finance, and supervise church-related institutions such as homes, hospitals, camps, colleges, seminaries, and retreat centers; to serve as a prophetic voice in the larger community; to serve as the basic building block for interchurch cooperation; to create, produce, and distribute educational resources; to provide continuing educational experiences for both the clergy and the laity; to operate pension systems for the clergy; to produce religious programming for transmission by radio and television; to propagate a specific doctrinal statement; to endorse or oppose legislative proposals in state legislatures and the United States Congress; to feed the hungry, clothe the naked, shelter the homeless, visit those in prison, and other acts of Christian mercy; to enlist and equip laypersons for fulltime Christian vocations; to create investment opportunities for people with discretionary wealth; and to collect and redistribute both income and wealth.

That is far from an exhaustive list. It is included here to illustrate one point. Today, literally thousands of congregations in American Protestantism are doing what formerly was done by denominational systems. That takes us back to the first of these three questions: Can United Methodists agree that the culture of this religious body must be transformed before meaningful changes can be made? If the response is in the affirmative, that raises the second question: What could be the most relevant and productive change in the culture of this denomination? From this observer's perspective the answer is clear. The culture should be changed from one designed to support a regulatory role for this denomination to a culture designed for the resourcing of congregations.

One of the most significant changes on the American ecclesiastical scene during the past half century has been the growing demand for relevance and excellence. This means it is far more difficult today to meet the expectations the generations born after 1950 bring to church than it was to meet the expectations of their parents and grandparents. One consequence is new missions often are open to "new ways to be church," while congregations founded before 1950 are tempted to "keep on doing what we've been doing the way we've always done it."

Another is the growing demand by congregational leaders for help. They seek help in designing a customized ministry plan, in equipping volunteer leaders, in fundraising, in switching from a producer-driven approach to Christian education to building learning communities, in affirming demographic diversity, in designing ministries with families that include teenagers, in feeding the spiritual hunger people bring to church, in challenging believers to become disciples, in building continuing relationships with sister churches on other continents, in creating experiential worship, in the use of projected visual imagery, in designing new physical facilities, in organizing ministries with new single parents, and in having scores of other aspects of ministry.

Do a majority of United Methodist policymakers agree the focus of the organizational structure should be changed from primarily a regulatory role to primarily on the resourcing of congregations?

That leads to the third and most challenging of these three questions. Will the United Methodist agencies, conferences, and districts be able to compete in what already is an exceptionally competitive marketplace? Will they be able to compete on both quality and price?

Currently, thousands of UM congregations are buying resources from a huge variety of non-UM vendors, including teaching churches, websites, parachurch organizations, independent publishing houses, retreat centers, seminaries, and others. Will the UM vendors be able to compete in that marketplace? Or, will they require a financial subsidy through apportionments in order to compete? Or, will renewed denominational loyalty make the UM vendors the preferred choice? Or, is the prudent course of action to continue to close more UM churches every year than are launched as new missions? Should we delete this scenario from the list of alternative possibilities?

XII. It's Easier the Second Time

Impatient readers born before 1830 with clear memories of the past probably will exclaim, "You're finally getting it right! The Methodists split in 1844, the United Brethren split in 1889, and the Evangelicals split in 1891—or some claim 1894. All three of our traditions discovered schism is the best way to respond to a highly divisive intradenominational quarrel. The time has come to learn from earlier generations. If those lines in the sand are so numerous, so wide, and so deep that reconciliation is impossible, maybe the time has come to split up and let each faction go its separate way. You suggested a process for this back in your third scenario in this chapter. Let's take another look at that option."

One objection to that suggestion is that few of today's policy-makers were born before 1830. They don't remember how it was done. The church historian explains, "That's not a problem. We can learn from history that we did not personally experience. One of our learnings from those three schisms is that the intensity of intradenominational quarreling prepares leaders to master the skills required for schism. These intradenominational quarrels have been going on for a long time. By now we should have hundreds, maybe thousands, of clergy and laity prepared for the logical next stage, which is schism. Look around. See how the Lutherans, Presbyterians, Baptists, and Episcopalians have used intradenominational quarreling as their version of spring training in preparation for the season when they play for keeps. If they build on their experiences to prepare for a new day, why can't the Methodists do the same?"

The logic of that paragraph is so persuasive that this scenario merits careful examination. If a long period of divisive intradenominational quarreling is the first stage in preparing for schism, what's the next step? This pilgrim is convinced that to minimize digging more lines in the sands and to accelerate the process, the next step should be to agree on what is non-negotiable. Chapter 5 of this book identifies four topics any reasonable umpire should be ready to affirm as items in a rulebook for schismatics.

A concurrent step could be "How do we design a process that will stimulate creativity, challenge the venturesome personalities, and open the door to new expressions of ministry?" The wrong answer is to offer each congregation three choices: (1) perpetuate the past, (2) a modest degree of change, and (3) radical change. That biases the agenda in favor of minimizing change. A better alternative is based on the assumption there are oceans of untapped creativity, challenging ideas, and relevant experiences in the hearts and minds of tens of thousands of congregational leaders in this denomination. A related assumption is that stream of creativity is larger and more powerful when it is challenged into creating the new rather than patching up the old.

A third assumption is that the right of self-determination is one of the most powerful themes in the world today. President Woodrow Wilson, the son and grandson of Presbyterian ministers, popularized that concept in an address he delivered to Congress on January 8, 1918. The famous "Fourteen Points" of that speech became guidelines in arriving at a peace treaty. For nine decades that right of self-determination has been a central driving force in the formulation of American foreign policy. It also has been a powerful motivating force in the creation of new denominations and tens of thousands of new nondenominational congregations under that broad umbrella called American Protestant Christianity. The right of self-determination also had influenced the creation of a growing number of liberation movements. Currently, the demand for that right is creating disruptive tensions within the Roman Catholic Church. It is a right that cannot be denied in planning for the future of The United Methodist Church in the United States.

A fourth assumption is based on the conviction that parents who have nurtured dependency in their children do not have a right to decide one day to walk away and abandon their dependent children. Likewise, a denomination that has fostered dependency among congregations does not have a right to suddenly abandon those dependent congregations. Therefore the list of alternatives for each congregation in this scenario should include at least these six options:

1. Pay the exit fee and choose your own future. (Exercise the right of self-determination.)

2. Pay the exit fee and affiliate with a new Methodist denomination with a new name that will closely resemble today's United Methodist Church in terms of its constitution, doctrine, polity, and culture, except for these five major differences: (a) the Restrictive Rules will be deleted from the constitution (the living, not the dead, will determine their future); (b) it will include only those congregations that choose to affiliate with it; (c) the name will *not* be The United Methodist Church; (d) those congregations that elect to help create it will determine criteria for defining the boundaries of the annual conferences; and (e) those annual conferences and congregations will determine the responsibilities and structure of the national agencies required to service this new denomination.

3. Pay the exit fee and help create a new Methodist denomination that will replicate The United Methodist Church in doctrine, but with a new polity, organizational structure, and system of accountability.

4. Pay the exit fee and help create a new Protestant denomination with its own distinctive doctrinal statement and an episcopal system of governance.

5. Pay the exit fee and help create a new Wesleyan denomination in which those designing it will define both the polity and doctrine.

6. Pay the exit fee and help create a new Christian religious body in America in which those designing it will define both the polity and doctrine.[11]

What will happen to the Central Conferences? Each one will be free to choose between becoming a completely autonomous conference and petitioning for affiliation with a denomination of its choice.

What will happen to the accumulated assets of the various annual conferences and national agencies? This could resemble that third scenario described earlier. The United Methodist Foundation, the United Methodist Board of Pensions, the Commission on Archives and History, and The United

Methodist Publishing House would continue as separate legal entities to service those constituencies that choose to utilize their services. The net assets resulting from the liquidation of the assets of the annual conferences could be used to help fund retirement benefits. The title to the net assets of the other national agencies could be transferred to the United Methodist Foundation, with instructions to distribute the funds among the Central Conferences to help them expand their evangelistic and missional ministries.

Is Compromise a Possibility?

This traveler's estimate is that in at least 30,000 United Methodist congregations in the United States the congregational leaders agree, "We don't have a dog in that fight. Why can't we just continue with the doctrine and polity in the UM constitution? We're comfortable here in the middle! Why can't those folks on the left and the right leave us alone? We're happy with the status quo."

That wish introduces the most widely followed response to intradenominational quarrels in American church history. This response also has been used in England, Germany, Korea, and scores of other countries. "If you're not happy with how things are going here, the door is wide open. Leave!" That response has produced at least 600 new denominations, conventions, associations, fellowships, and conferences in American Protestantism since 1750.

A special session of the General Conference could be called for 2006 to act on two proposals. The first would be a declaration that The United Methodist Church will continue with its present constitution, doctrine, and polity without amendment until at least 2024. By that date most of the current discontented members of this denomination will have moved to a non-UM congregation or to a nursing home or to their favorite cemetery or to a columbarium. (This writer promises to choose one of those options by 2020.)

If the declaration to affirm the status quo is adopted, that will enable those who so desire to continue as members of The United Methodist Church. The second proposal would be that with 60 percent approval of all resident members present and voting at a properly called congregational meeting, any congregation that so desires may withdraw from this denomination. If the members wished to retain title to the tangible and intangible assets of that congregation, they may do so by payment of a fair and equitable exit fee to compensate for what that congregation did not contribute in earlier years. This could mean the congregation founded in 1900 that currently includes 200 full members would pay a higher exit fee than the 200-member church organized in 1980.

This window of opportunity to withdraw would be open from January 1, 2008, through December 31, 2009. That would give every conference at least a year or more to compute that total unfunded liability for retirement benefits and to arrive at a fair and equitable exit fee for each congregation. It also would give each congregation more than a year to discuss the probable consequences of continuing its affiliation with The United Methodist Church, as well as the probable consequences of withdrawing. Obviously the exit fee would be a factor in those discussions, but it would be clear that sooner or later the presence of that elephant in the chancel must be recognized. The choice would be, "Do we feed that malnourished elephant now or later?"

Most important, however, delaying the opening of that window until January 1, 2008, or perhaps until July 1, 2008, would give the policymakers in both the national agencies and the annual conferences time to prepare a ministry plan for the following five to seven years. Those ministry plans would provide each congregation with a valuable resource in making their decisions. In essence, these customized ministry plans would communicate to each congregation, "This is what we plan to do in ministry over the next five years. Do you want to continue your partnership with us in implementing this plan?"

Scores of congregations might look at the ministry plan of their current annual conference, compare it with the ministry plan of conference B, and decide to switch to a new partner. Would that be permitted? With two reservations, this pilgrim's answer would be, "Of course!" One reservation is this must be a two-way street. To be allowed to continue its affiliation with its current conference, or to apply for admission into another conference, every congregation would be required to prepare and submit its own five-year ministry plan as part of its application. Unless agreement can be reached within ninety days after submission of that application, each conference will be free to reject the application from any congregation.

The other reservation, of course, is every congregation would be required to pay its exit fee or agree to a payment schedule for that fee before it would be permitted to submit any proposal for its future to anyone. Deadlines can be useful in helping both individuals and institutions focus their thinking on the future and the probable consequences of each potential course of action.

This variation on a total schism would allow those who want to perpetuate The United Methodist Church under its current name and with the current constitution to do so. It also could push to the periphery most of the pressures that have motivated the current wave of intradenominational quarreling. Most important of all, it has the potential to push planning for ministry in the first fifteen years of this new millennium to the top of the agenda in every congregation and every annual conference. By requiring conferences to earn the allegiance of congregations, this could be an effective antidote to the continued spread of disengagement. For those born before 1950 a major fringe benefit could be the funding of those promised retirement benefits.

Is this a dream, or could it really happen? A response to that question depends on four variables. First, is it realistic to expect a slow-moving and dysfunctional institution to be able to make the decisions required to produce a workable compromise? Or, is the temporary comfort of denial so powerful that it will continue to immobilize the policy-making processes? Given a choice between denial or a continued aging and melting of that United Methodist ice cube, will denial win the most votes? From this observer's perspective the most serious crisis in this denomination is not the quarrel between the progressives and the conservatives over biblical interpretation. The urgent crisis is the conflict between those who find comfort in the fact the glass is still half full, and those who are concerned about the future because the glass is half empty.

Second, is the fear of "creeping congregationalism" so pervasive that it would block any proposal to grant congregational leaders meaningful choices beyond paying or not paying apportionments?

Third, is the widespread reluctance to utilize modern technology so great that implementation of this compromise would require ten years rather than two? For example, a crucial component for turning this possible compromise into reality would be for every conference to announce on its website every Friday afternoon the current version of its ministry plan for the future. Which conference would be the first to post the final version of its ministry plan? Which conference would be the last? Which plan would attract the most early applications from congregations? Which conferences would declare "We'll accept any congregation that applies?" Could a cluster of fifty "Old First Church Downtown" congregations join together and create a website that declares "This is who we are, and this is what we believe God is calling us to do in ministry in the twenty-first century. Which conference wants to receive our packet of applications?"

Finally, implementation of this compromise would require affirmation of a practice in the Methodist Episcopal Church of a hundred years ago. A century ago that branch of American Methodism operated on the assumption that a denomination could offer congregations a choice between membership in a geographically defined annual conference or in a nongeographical affinity conference. Implementation of this compromise would require legitimatizing that practice. The door would be open for any of the currently geographically defined annual conferences to reinvent itself as a nongeographical affinity conference if that was an essential characteristic of its ministry plan for the twenty-first century.

Do you believe competition and choices could stimulate creativity and raise the level of quality? What other scenarios for the future of The United Methodist Church should be added this list? Do you see a better way to spark creativity, to reverse disengagement, to build a strong future orientation into each congregation, and to improve accountability to the constituents?

Or, do you prefer denial? Or, are you so addicted to the sport of intradenominational quarreling you cannot break that addiction? Or, would you prefer to help your congregation pay its annual franchise tax (currently described as apportionments) and concentrate the rest of your discretionary time, energy, prayers, creativity, and money on helping to strengthen and expand the ministry of your congregation? Or, is that not on the list of options in a connectional polity?

NOTES

Introduction

1. Leon Howell, *United Methodism @ Risk: A Wake-up Call* (Kingston, N.Y.: Information Project for United Methodists, 2003).
2. James Nuechterlein, "Athens and Jerusalem in Indiana," *The American Scholar* (Summer 1988): 353-68. Professor Nuechterlein recalls that he was introduced to this metaphor by the president of Valparaiso University, Otto Paul Kretzmann, who declared that the university was located at the intersection of Athens and Jerusalem and represented "the fusion of high learning and high religion" (p. 355).
3. For an earlier and detailed analysis of this strategy, see Norman M. Green and Paul W. Light, "Growth and Decline in an Inclusive Denomination: The ABC Experience," in *Church and Denominational Growth*, edited by David A. Roozen and C. Kirk Hadaway (Nashville: Abingdon Press, 1993), 112-26.
4. George M. Marsden and Bradley J. Longfield, eds., *The Secularization of the Academy* (New York: Oxford University Press, 1992).
5. Those statistics for 1956 are from Yoshio Fukuyama, "Non-theological Aspects of Church Union: The Institutional Formation of the United Church of Christ," in *The United Church of Christ: Studies in Identity and Polity*, edited by Dorothy C. Bass and Kenneth B. Smith (Chicago: Exploration Press, 1987), 39.
6. James Turner, *Without God, Without Creed: The Origins of Unbelief in America* (Baltimore: The Johns Hopkins University Press, 1985).

7. Among the most useful have been William H. Willimon and Robert L. Wilson, *Rekindling the Flame* (Nashville: Abingdon Press, 1987); Andy Langford and William H. Willimon, *A New Connection* (Nashville: Abingdon Press, 1995); Jackson Carroll and Wade Clark Roof, eds., *Beyond Establishment* (Louisville: Westminster/John Knox Press, 1993); Christian Smith, *American Evangelicalism: Embattled and Thriving* (Chicago: University of Chicago Press, 1998); Wade Clark Roof and William McKinney, *American Mainline Religion* (New Brunswick, N.J.: Rutgers University Press, 1987); Robert Wuthnow, *The Restructuring of American Religion* (Princeton: Princeton University Press, 1988); Michael Slaughter, *The Learning Church* (Loveland, Colo.: Group Publishing, Inc., 2002); Donald E. Miller, *Reinventing American Protestantism* (Berkeley: University of California Press, 1997); Robert William Fogel, *The Fourth Great Awakening* (Chicago: University of Chicago Press, 2000); G. A. Pritchard, *Willow Creek Seeker Services* (Grand Rapids, Mich.: Baker Books, 1996); Rob Weber, *Visual Leadership* (Nashville: Abingdon Press, 2002); Paul E. Johnson, ed., *African-American Christianity* (Berkeley: University of California Press, 1994); Adam Hamilton, *Leading Beyond the Walls* (Nashville: Abingdon Press, 2002); Keith B. Brown, *On the Road Again* (New York: Church Publishing, 2001); Marsha G. Witten, *All Is Forgiven* (Princeton: Princeton University Press, 1993); and B. Joseph Pine and James H. Gilmore, *The Experience Economy* (Boston: Harvard Business School Press, 1999).

8. See Lyle E. Schaller, *Tattered Trust* (Nashville: Abingdon Press, 1996), and Lyle E. Schaller, "Is Schism the Next Step?" *Circuit Rider* (September/October 1998): 4-5.

9. An excellent introduction to the earlier stages of this battle over control can be found in Russell E. Richey, *The Methodist Conference in America* (Nashville: Abingdon Press, 1996), 185-98.

10. The story of how the commitment to spread scriptural holiness across the land could be combined with God, mother, flag, and class meetings to produce a unified and rapidly growing religious body that eventually became bureaucratized is told by A. Gregory Schneider, *The Way of the Cross Leads Home* (Bloomington: Indiana University Press, 1993).

1. The Melting of Our Ice Cube

1. The membership-to-population ratios for 1771 and 1816 are from Charles W. Ferguson, *Organizing to Beat the Devil* (New York: Doubleday & Company, 1971), 54. The ratios for 1890, 1906, 1916, and 1926 were calculated from data in the four censuses of religious bodies conducted by the United States Bureau of the Census in those four years. The ratios for 1950 and later are based on the reports by American annual conferences on confirmed membership, plus the number on the preparatory roll.

2. Richard P. Deitzler, "A Comprehensive Look at How Average Worship Attendance (AWA) and Average Sunday School Attendance (ASSA) Have Occurred from 1994 to 1999 Among All UMC Churches and Jurisdictions in United States" (Fayetteville, N.Y.: May 8, 2001).

3. A superb introduction to the proliferation of foundations in recent American history is Eleanor L. Brilliant, *Private Charity and Public Inquiry: A History of the Filer and Peterson Commissions* (Bloomington: Indiana University Press, 2000).

4. The use of giving circles is described by Lyle E. Schaller, *The New Context for Ministry* (Nashville: Abingdon Press, 2003), 277.

5. That conflict in spending between necessities and discretionary expenditures is the theme of Elizabeth Warren and Amelia Warren Tyagi, *The Two-income Trap* (New York: Basic Books, 2003).

6. For an exceptionally well-written book on the use of statistics in evaluating outcomes in annual performance reviews, see Michael Lewis, *Moneyball* (New York: W. W. Norton, 2003). The crucial point is the distinction between focusing on inputs such as credentials and placing greater value on outcomes.

7. The combined EUB and Methodist membership statistics for 1960 are from *General Minutes of the Annual Conferences of The United Methodist Church 1972* (Evanston: The Council on Finance and Administration, 1972), 28.

8. The state-by-state membership statistics for 2000 are based on Dale E. Jones et al., *Religious Congregations & Membership in the United States 2000* (Nashville: Glenmary Research Center, 2002). In several states, these reported membership figures vary slightly from those reported in the *General Minutes 2001* for calendar 2000.

9. An earlier comprehensive survey of the research on the shrinking presence of mainstream Protestantism is Milton J. Coalter, John M. Mulder, and Louis B. Weeks, *Vital Signs* (Grand Rapids, Mich.: William B. Eerdmans Publishing Company, 1996). For interesting and relevant discussions of the internal turmoil in two other religious bodies in America, see Peter Steinfels, *A People Adrift* (New York: Simon & Schuster, 2003) for a discussion of the liberal-conservative division in American Catholicism. The author contends the choice is between decline and transformation. The recent rapid increase in the role of women in American Catholic parishes is one of the themes of David Gibson, *The Coming Catholic Church* (San Francisco: HarperSanFrancisco, 2003). The mounting expectations placed on the Jewish rabbi is the theme of Jack Wertheimer, "The Rabbi Crisis," *Commentary* (May 2003): 35-39. Even more interesting are the eleven letters to the editor spread over nine pages in response to Wertheimer's article in the September 2003 issue of *Commentary*.

10. Intradenominational quarreling is one of the factors offered to explain the recent decrease in denominational receipts in the Southern Baptist Convention. See Mark Wingfield, "Churches Keep Greater Share at Home," *Baptist Standard* (August 25, 2003): 1, 6, 7.

2. How Many Lines in the Sand?

1. An excellent introduction to this debate is W. Stephen Gunter et al., *Wesley and the Quadrilateral* (Nashville: Abingdon Press, 1997).
2. A comprehensive description of the rise of the Unitarian movement and the consequences for the Congregationalists in New England can be found in Peter S. Field, *The Crisis of the Standing Order* (Amherst: University of Massachusetts Press, 1998). This was an early example of an intradenominational quarrel over authority and control.
3. For a quick introduction to the perspective of Bishop Spong, see John Shelby Spong, *Resurrection: Myth or Reality?* (San Francisco: Harper SanFrancisco, 1995), 233-60. For a more comprehensive account of this priest's rise from relative obscurity to world fame, see John Shelby Spong, *A New Christianity for a New World* (San Francisco: HarperSanFrancisco, 2001).
4. A more broadly focused discussion on the contemporary influence of renewal groups is Michael S. Hamilton and Jennifer McKinney, "Turning the Mainline Around," *Christianity Today* (August 2003): 34-40.
5. A provocative introduction to this subject is Aaron Wildavsky, *The Rise of Radical Individualism* (Washington, D.C.: The American University Press, 1991). Those who are puzzled by the attractiveness of nondenominational congregations will benefit from reading Robert H. Wiebe, *Self-rule: A Cultural History of American Democracy* (Chicago: University of Chicago Press, 1995). Political liberals will enjoy Herbert J. Gans, *Middle American Individualism* (New York: Oxford University Press, 1988).
6. For a different set of categories for classifying congregations, see Lyle E. Schaller, *What Have We Learned?* (Nashville: Abingdon Press, 2001), 166-87.
7. An excellent introduction to the characteristics of a voluntary association is J. Roland Pennock and John W. Chapman, eds., *Voluntary Associations* (New York: Atherton Press, 1969).
8. For informed insider reflections on this subject, see Daniel P. Moynihan, *Maximum Feasible Misunderstanding* (New York: The Free Press, 1969). This observer's contemporary reflections on this subject can be found in Lyle E. Schaller, *The Churches' War on Poverty* (Nashville: Abingdon Press, 1967), 94-128.
9. For a brief discussion of the causes of "powerless hatred," see Pierre Manet, "Modern Democracy as a System of Separations," *Journal of Democracy* (January 2003): 114-25.

10. For a more detailed analysis of the size of congregations in American Protestantism, see Lyle E. Schaller, *Small Congregation, Big Potential* (Nashville: Abingdon Press, 2003). This author is convinced that one of the most influential factors in determining the future of The United Methodist Church will be the choice between the northern operational policy of increasing the number of small congregations and the southern operational policy of increasing the number of large congregations.

11. The affinity judicatory and the role of the teaching church are the two central themes of Lyle E. Schaller, *From Geography to Affinity: How Congregations Can Learn from One Another* (Nashville: Abingdon Press, 2003).

12. An excellent introduction to one version of the multisite option is J. Timothy Ahlen and J. V. Thomas, *One Church, Many Congregations* (Nashville: Abingdon Press, 1999). Another version is described in Eric Reed, "The New Video Preacher Experiment," *Leadership* (Spring 2003): 76-84. The partnership model between the small congregation and the large church is described in Schaller, *Small Congregation, Big Potential*, chapters 6 and 7.

3. What Do You Believe?

1. A summary of this report is in Peter Steinfels, "Beliefs," *The New York Times* (August 16, 2003): A10. The book was published by Church Publishing, Inc., in the summer of 2003.

2. This discussion draws heavily on Frederick A. Norwood, *The Story of American Methodism* (Nashville: Abingdon Press, 1974), 376-80.

3. Those who want to explore in more depth the history, evolution, culture, and characteristics of voluntary associations could begin with the collection of essays edited by J. Roland Pennock and John W. Chapman, *Voluntary Associations* (New York: Atherton Press, 1969).

4. Those who believe the UMC can and should be reinvented as a high-expectation, high-commitment Christian covenant community, and are looking for clues on what that could resemble would do well to read Thomas E. Ricks, *Making the Corps* (New York: Scribner, 1997).

5. See note 5 in chapter 2.

6. For a discussion of a widely discussed internal quarrel in a major university, see James Traub, "Harvard Radical," *New York Times Magazine* (August 24, 2003): 48ff. The road to revolutionizing a big institution is paved with ill will, resistance, and hostility.

7. This observer's brief for creating affinity conferences as a way to enhance learning is found in Schaller, *From Geography to Affinity*.

8. This reference is to Roger G. Barker and Paul V. Gump, *Big School, Small*

Notes

School (Stanford: Stanford University Press, 1994). For a discussion of the larger concept, see Roger G. Barker, *Ecological Psychology* (Stanford: Stanford University Press, 1968). For this traveler's summary of the impact of the ecological environment, see Lyle E. Schaller, *The Evolution of the American Public High School* (Nashville: Abingdon Press, 2000), 62-96.

9. While many Christians deplore the fact that American churches do compete with one another for future constituents, that is a part of contemporary reality. For a long-term analysis of this fact of ecclesiastical life, see Roger Finke and Rodney Stark, *The Churching of America 1776–1990: Winners and Losers in Our Religious Economy* (New Brunswick, N.J.: Rutgers University Press, 1992).

10. For an introduction to the contributions of Deming, see Mary Walton, *The Deming Management Method* (New York: Perigee Books, 1986).

11. For a more detailed discussion of this strategy for the transformation of lives, see Schaller, *What Have We Learned?* pp. 119-23.

4. Six Other Perspectives

1. Daniel K. Church, "The Church in Transition," *Worship Arts* (September/October 2003): 4.
2. T. S. Eliot, "The Hollow Men" (1925).

6. Many Roads into the Future

1. Ahlen and Thomas, *One Church, Many Congregations*, 77-93.
2. The multisite option is described in Lyle E. Schaller, *Innovations in Ministry* (Nashville: Abingdon Press, 1994), 98-133.
3. This option is described in Schaller, *Small Congregations, Big Potential*, chapter 7.
4. J. William T. Youngs, Jr., *God's Messengers: Religious Leadership in Colonial New England* (Baltimore: Johns Hopkins University Press, 1976), 143.
5. Methodist opposition to federal dollars going directly to public schools is recalled in Robert Moats Miller, *Bishop G. Bromley Oxnam: Paladin of Liberal Protestantism* (Nashville: Abingdon Press, 1990), 430-34. Oxnam's fear, of course, was that could lead to the allocation of tax dollars to private schools. The irony of the debate is that while it was a divisive public policy issue, tens of thousands of veterans were using tax dollars to pay their tuition bills at private colleges, universities, and theological schools. The Roman Catholic position was that, since millions of those tax dollars were being paid by Roman Catholics with children enrolled in private schools, those private schools should be eligible for those grants.

7. Repair or Replace?

1. This distinction between one's private life and the public realm is the theme of an essay by English Anglican priest Peter Mullen, "The Last Straw," *The Wall Street Journal* (August 26, 2003): A12.
2. An introduction to the perspective of Donald McGavran, who founded the church growth movement, is in Roozen and Hadaway, *Church Denominational Growth*, pp. 142-43.
3. Donald L. Horowitz, "The Cracked Foundations of the Right to Secede," *Journal of Democracy* (April 2003): 5-17.
4. This option is described in Schaller, *Small Congregation, Big Potential*, chapters 6 and 7.
5. Manet, "Modern Democracy as a System of Separations," 114-25.
6. An extensive essay on this subject is Jonathan Chait, "The Case for Bush Hatred: Mad About You," *The New Republic* (September 29, 2003): 20-24.
7. Russell E. Richey and Thomas Edward Frank, *Episcopacy in the Methodist Tradition: Perspectives and Proposals* (Nashville: Abingdon Press, 2004).
8. The assumption that every elder, deacon, and local pastor is obligated to "uphold the doctrines and theological teachings" of The United Methodist Church is stated very clearly in Elaine A. Robinson, "Preaching Methodist Doctrine," *Quarterly Review* (Winter 2002): 401.
9. This ancient organizing principle is described in Lyle E. Schaller, *Community Organization: Conflict and Reconciliation* (Nashville: Abingdon Press, 1966), 90-114.
10. An excellent book that describes the larger context for recent quarreling is James Davison Hunter, *Culture Wars: The Struggle to Define America* (New York: Basic Books, 1991).
11. Why do five of these alternatives include the expectation that a new denomination must have its own doctrinal statement? The heart of this issue was expressed in seventeen words in a book review essay: "Whatever some Christians may think about them, creeds get people thinking clearly about issues that really matter" (William C. Placher, "Why Creeds Matter: Believe It or Not," *Christian Century* [September 20, 2003]: 20-24). In the conclusion of that highly relevant essay, Professor Placher comments, "Creeds and confessions can function either to establish a consensus or to make clear lines of disagreement . . . if the next generation does not find a way of establishing consensus, it may be necessary to draw dividing lines" (p. 24).